MacDuff's

The Construction and Reconstruction of St Drostan's Church Markinch

Bruce F. Manson

2016

Pittanhaigles Press

© Bruce F. Manson 2017

ISBN 978-0-9955580-0-7

Front cover design by Bob Marshall

Introduction

The 12th century saw the Scotland that we know today begin to emerge as the descendants of Margaret and Malcolm III pushed the boundaries of the realm beyond Alba and retreated from claims north of the Tees. The charter evidence for this period is not strong and we must use every scrap of available information if we are to understand the complex inter-relationships existing within a multilingual and multi-ethnic nation defining itself in many ways with respect to its larger neighbour to the south.

At the heart of this growing nation was Fife, ancestral home of the MacDuff Earls, a dynasty with special privileges, close to the Scottish throne. Despite their proximity to royalty, the MacDuffs' ancestral heartland was under pressure from energetic Abbots in Dunfermline protecting their royal privileges and from equally royally privileged bishops in St Andrews. The response of the earls as the century wore on was to develop a wider landowning base across Scotland as a whole but the family itself stayed rooted within their traditional homelands. David I ensured that Anglo-Norman patterns of succession in exchange for knight service took the place of the old Gaelic *tànaiste* system and a line of earls inheriting between father and son established itself in Fife. The old system of clan leadership by acclaim within the kinship group seems to have lived on in parallel to the earldom, surfacing when an earl was in his minority and preserving the title "MacDuff" until well into the 14th century. Does the epithet "MacDuff's Kirk" applied to the 12th century church of Markinch in 19th century writings have any basis in fact or is it a relatively recently coined fiction? The following pages examine a remarkable church building in the heart of MacDuff territory and within a short distance of their ancient place of legal assembly.

The correct reading of a building may yield as much, if not more than a charter, a factual record of legal interest. A building is an expression of the patron's power, pride and faith. It is the end product of the master builder's skill and imagination. Its stones bear the tool marks of native and itinerant workmen. Its layout and decoration reflect the rituals of its clergy. Ecclesiastical buildings represent the greatest artistic achievements of the medieval period and were the natural targets of those intent on effacing all traces of the old order. Scotland is a country that went through a violent and iconoclastic Reformation. Markinch was close to the heart of this revolution and yet enough of the town's old kirk remains to demonstrate that it was once a striking statement of both faith and construction technology, eclipsed until recently by the spectacular national monuments built during the same century at Dunfermline and St Andrews.

This study focusses upon the many puzzles surrounding the 12th century remains of Markinch Church but it attempts to trace the history of the building beyond that period up until relatively recently. It asks how a church that was once a high, narrow Romanesque monument, most probably painted with biblical images, illuminated by candlelight, infused with the smell of incense and scattered with gilded family tombs, came to be transformed into the bright and elegant Georgian building that is used for worship today.

This study is a reconstruction. It attempts to take a forensic approach to examining the evidence that remains. What has been removed from the scene? What has been tampered with and why should some of the clues have been left intact? What can other 12th century buildings tell us about its likely appearance? It is what Warwick Rodwell calls the 360 degree approach to church investigation, drawing upon archaeology, manuscript sources, architectural history, political history and above all empirical observation[1]. It relies upon expertise from a number of related disciplines and a dedicated team of volunteers. It does not pretend to be an academic treatise but it is hoped that a thorough study of a single building will contribute in a small way toward an overall understanding of 11th and 12th century building practice within the wider picture of power structures in Northern Britain.

With respected to the use of technical terminology, an attempt is made wherever possible to use technical terms alongside their commonly understood alternatives. Hopefully this clarifies matters for professional and general reader alike and avoids the need to refer constantly to a glossary.

As regards the anonymous 12th century builder or builders, in the absence of a set of invoices and title deeds, can we profile the likely candidates from the few manuscript sources that remain after so many hundreds of years? It is true that we have copies of documents showing a transfer of ownership to the Priory of St Andrews over a period of many decades but how selective were the records that were kept? Do the donation charters of 1166/67 refer to

[1] Rodwell, W., 2012, *The Archaeology of Churches*, Amberley

an ageing building, a very ancient building or to a new one, and was it a gift as we understand the term? Fortunately recent research has helped to shed light upon the 12th century Fife aristocracy and the following chapters owe a debt to that work.[2]

Acknowledgements

This publication is drawn up with the financial support of the Strathmartine Trust and represents the fourth in a series of progress reports written within the framework of the Living Lomonds Landscape Partnership, a Heritage Lottery Funded Programme begun in August 2013. The author is supported by a team of volunteers drawn from the Archaeological Sub-Committee of Markinch Heritage Group. Other funders include the Hunter Archaeological and Historical Trust, Fife Environment Trust, Fife Council and Historic Environment Scotland. Valuable contributions in kind have been received from RCAHMS along with advice from Historic Scotland and CARTA, the Church of Scotland's Architectural advisory body. The Kirk Session of Markinch and Thornton Parish Church led by John Wood, Session

[2] Taylor, Dr S. with Márcus, G. The Place-Names of Fife. Vols II & V (referred to hereafter as PNF II & PNF V).

Clerk and the Fabrics Committee Chaired by Robert Balfour have provided support throughout. Thanks are due also to Dr Oliver O'Grady whose contribution with ground penetrating radar and geophysical surveying in year 1 has been invaluable and to Moira Greig MIfA, FSA (Scot) who conducted an extensive survey of masons' marks in year 3 along with a team of volunteers. Advice and encouragement from Douglas Speirs, Regional Archaeologist is also much appreciated, and the survey work on the tower by Dr Mhairi-Claire Semple served as an inspiration.[3]

Particular thanks are due to the hard work of Neil Sutherland Chair of Markinch Heritage Group for proof-reading and financial management, Maureen Brand for manuscript research, Gavin Brown, Church Officer, James Jack and other members of the Church Archaeology Sub-committee. Michael Brand provided specialist lighting equipment for some of the interior images. All contributed ideas that are scattered throughout the following pages.

Illustrations and plans are reproduced with kind permission of the Special Collections Department of St Andrews University Library, the National Records of Scotland and the former Royal Commission on Ancient and Historical Monuments (now part of Historic Environment Scotland). The artist responsible for the front cover and several internal illustrations is Bob Marshall.

Finally, we are grateful for the many observations made by a wide range of people either during the various open days held over the three year period or in response to drafts of annual reports. These include, in no particular order, Professor John Hume, Gilbert Màrkus, Professor Richard Fawcett, Professor Richard Oram, Professor David Munro, Dr Richard Gem, Professor Eric Fernie, Dr Iain Anderson, Dr. Alex Woolf and especially Professor Barbara Crawford and Dr Simon Taylor. The views expressed in this document are, of course, entirely the responsibility of the author[4].

Bruce F. Manson MA (Hons), MSc. FSA (Scot)

[3] Semple, Dr M-C. 2009 The towers of Alba

[4] The author studied History of Architecture as part of a wider undergraduate degree but took a Masters Degree in Urban Design and Regional Planning. He taught for a short while as a Research Fellow at Edinburgh University before pursuing a career in Local Government

1. The Medieval Markinch Landscape

Lochs, myres, knowes and inches

A project that emerges out of a Landscape Partnership[5] should fittingly begin with a description of the underlying geology and topography of the land around Markinch. The original place of worship (and there may have been several, both Christian and pre-Christian) would have been built upon a mound close to the mouth of a stream that flowed into a long loch stretching to the east. There is no doubt that this kind of elevated position close to still or running water was a favoured position for the siting of a place of worship in early Christian Scotland and may even have its origins well before that era. Other examples include St Vigeans in Angus and St Magridins near Abdie.

This loch has gradually silted up over the past two thousand years but was known as the Myres until extensive drainage took place in the 18th and 19th centuries. In times of flooding the extent of the loch can still be seen. Both the mound and the loch were formed by glaciers from the north and west grinding away the natural bedrock and depositing their contents when they melted. The stream had its origins in marshes close to the summit of East Lomond and once spilled into the Loch, barely one hundred yards from the church. Here, where we now have the marshes of the Glebe, small fishing boats may once have been tied up and the loch may well have been navigable as far as Balcurvie near Windygates. The loch and the marsh have now been fully drained and the view to the east is obscured by a railway embankment running in a north-south direction just to the east of the church's 13th century glebe lands.

Location and links to the rest of Fife

The so-called Markinch Gap between the Lomonds and the higher land to the east would have been on a north-south communication route from earliest times. The choice of routes was further constrained by Balfarg Loch

---

[5] The Living Lomonds Landscape Partnership, a Heritage Lottery funded programme

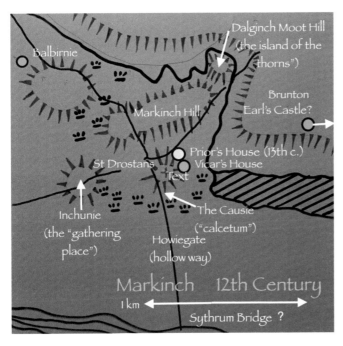

Dalginch Moot Hill
(the island of the
thorns")

Balbirnie

Brunton
Earl's Castle?

Markinch Hill

Prior's House (13th c.)
St Drostans
Vicar's House

Text

The Causie

Inchunie
("calcetum")

(the "gathering
place")

Howiegate
(hollow way)

Markinch 12th Century

1 km

Sythrum Bridge ?

to the north where the peatlands of Star Moss now lie. To the west, the place-name Auchmuty suggests a fording place across the Leven close to the present day Balbirnie Bridge and old roads point to another crossing point immediately to the south of Markinch near Sythrum.

During the period of the Viking invasions there would have been a distinct advantage in a place of worship being located so far away from the coast in a complex landscape of treacherous marshes and sinuous lochs. Markinch could have been one of several Pictish churches that retreated inland during the 9th century. Alternatively, a Pictish church could have been located close to a place of worship dating back to the time of the henge monument at nearby Balfarg. The answer may lie under the pews at the east end of the present day church and this possibility is discussed further in the next chapter.

The road leading to the church from the west crossed over Inchunie (*inch aonach* or the *gathering place?*) where there is now a caravan park. The route from the north east passed along the shoulder of Cuinan Hill on its way to Kennoway and St Andrews. To the north west the pathway most probably passed by Stobcross on its way to Balfarg. At some point in the medieval period Markinch was split into three divisions, East, West and Nether. All were probably once within the wider barony of Dalginch, itself part of the Shire of Strathleven, a very early feudal division now reflected in the extensive parish of Markinch.

Underlying Geology

Whoever built the 12th century church would have found all their requirements within a mile or so. Close to the surface are sandstone beds, associated with layers of limestone and seams of outcropping coal. Freestone, sand and lime would have been essential building materials. A piece of land close to Markinch was known as Limepotts up until the early 19th century and the First Statistical Account refers to "beds of marl" being excavated at Balbirnie. Two main sandstone quarries, marked with a star on map 2) were also used up until the 19th century. These were Sythrum which once produced a hard, veined stone but in its latter stages could only provide a softer, iron-rich material. There also appears to have been a stone quarry at Northhall as shown on an 18th century estate map. Present day deeds refer to the land as *Hole Acre* and it is possible that the name refers to stone quarrying activity or surface mining. Chips of coal were found embedded in the 12th century mortar of the tower.

A metal working forge would have been required to keep the masons' tools tempered and sharpened. Despite the lack of direct documentary evidence it is difficult to believe that coal from an outcrop running north south through Markinch was not used even as early as the 12th century. A charter of 1224 divides the teinds or produce of the land known as *Pitenchagal* (*the share of the church*) between Markinch Church and the earl's priest at Kilgour near Falkland.[6] The land, later known as Pittenhaggles most probably ran along the southern face of Markinch Hill between the church and Northhall. It was recorded separately along with Inchunie in the Brunton estate charters down through the medieval period most probably because of its mineral significance. According to the outcome of the 1224 agreement, Markinch was allocated the corn and all other produce but Kilgour was to have what remained. It is likely that this residual produce from the land was in fact its mineral rights whether they were coal or stone. If so then it is the earliest reference to mineral extraction in Scotland.

The monks of Soutra Aisle south of Edinburgh certainly had recorded mining interests in Markinch parish from an early time mentioned several times in the records of Trinity College Edinburgh.[7] Additionally, the russet coloured sandstone has a high iron content and again, early iron-working is a likelihood in the vicinity. Nearby Balgonie (G. *baile ghobhin*) means the *farm of the smiths* in Gaelic[8]. It is located within yards of a major coal outcrop. The

[6] PNF II p. 451

[7] Charters of the Hospital of Soltre, of Trinity College Edinburgh. Bannatyne Club 1862 pp 10, 46, 77

[8] PNF II p. 408

Gaelic language was, most likely, rapidly disappearing in the area by the 13th century and the place-name may be another indication of the antiquity of coal mining in the area despite the absence of written records. To sum up, the geology of the area provided all the requisite resources for a 12th century building project on a major scale. It required, however, the manpower strength and financial resources to import the necessary specialist skills to make full use of what was available. This element is explored in later chapters.

Where the ice had scraped down to the bedrock there were boggy areas overlying the impervious rocks. The higher, drier, areas were known locally as either *drums, knowes* or *inches*. Markinch is one of three *inches* in the vicinity, the others being Inchunie on the south eastern edge of the Balbirnie estate and Dalginch, most probably the cemetery mound at Northhall.[9] Markinch Hill itself is part of a sandy ridge that has been extensively shaped by human action, particularly along the northern flanks where great terraces have been formed by human effort for a purpose that is still a mystery. Sand was used as a resource within the local building industry during the 18th and 19th centuries when it was extracted from the south side of Markinch Hill. During the 12th century the southern flanks of the Hill were probably in the hands of the church (known as *The Holy Ground* in the 19th century) and their south and east facing aspect would have provided valuable revenue. It is possible that sand for the church building project was extracted from the less productive north-facing slopes. It would have been delivered by ox-cart and either dumped as foundation material or mixed in with the lime close to the building site. However, whether large cartloads were extracted to provide level foundations or to augment the size of the hill upon which the church is built is an open question. The terraces are wide enough to have taken ox-drawn carts but this theory is one of several relating to these enigmatic features.[10] It would have been a remarkable engineering feat but no more remarkable than the construction of the motte and seven defensive ditches at Maiden Castle on the eastern fringes of the parish.

The tower of the church that emerged from this landscape can still be seen today. The consistent use down through the ages of local honey-coloured, ochre and grey sandstone has blended several reconstructions and repairs

[9] PNF II   p 226

[10] Manson, Bruce 2008 *The Terraces of Markinch Hill.* (unpub.)

into an attractive amalgam of styles that has changed little since the last major phase of reconstruction in the 1880s. Closer inspection of the sandstone blocks reveals considerable variation in shade and texture that may give clues as the quarries where the stone was sourced.

Surface Features

The retreating glaciers dumped large quantities of sand and gravel all over the Markinch area and the church sits on top of one of these mounds, almost completely surrounded by marshland. Through this complex landscape flowed a stream, beginning in the Lomonds as the Coul and Conland Burns, flowing past the Neolithic and Bronze Age complex at Balfarg and through what is now Balbirnie Park. It would originally have meandered close to the back of Markinch Hill, looped around Northhall cemetery mound before cutting south through a gap in the ridge between that mound and the Cuinan Hill. The stream passes close to the church where it now turns east ending as the Back Burn, a drainage channel following the line of the old loch towards Windygates.

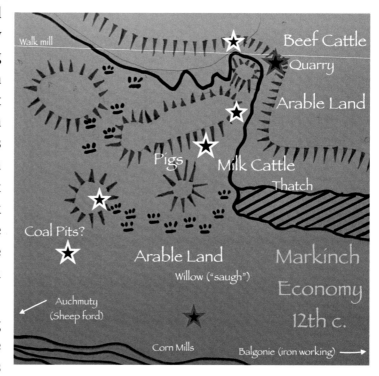

It is worth noting that although the Balfarg Henge was extensively excavated in the 1980s there has been no attempt to consider the significance to the early settlers of the entire landscape and the stream that runs through it. It is more than likely, however, that Balfarg, Dalginch/ Northhall, Markinch Hill and the mound upon which the church is built would have had a close relationship with each other from earliest times, each with a strong symbolic or practical significance to the area's inhabitants. This was an ancient landscape, much altered by human activity, long before the Gaels or even the Picts set foot in the territory.

By the medieval period some limited drainage would have taken place, with a 1286 charter of William de Valoniis referring to a fosse or ditch to the south of the kirkton, but marshland would have remained an important part of the local economy.[11] When land was distributed amongst estates it was carefully apportioned. Over the burn to the east of the church were three butts (ploughed ridges), three myres (portions of marshland) and three stretches of loch, all carefully demarcated in charters.[12] On the southern side of the marshland there were long cultivated strips known as *riggs* or *tongues*, and land was referred to as being on the shady side or the sunny side of a slope. Occasionally, odd triangular pieces of land were called *gushets*. We know that oak trees once grew in the area as there are records of large oaks being dug out of Star Moss but how many remained by the medieval period is difficult to judge. There may have been some limited managed woodland and we have evidence of pig production in the 12th century. The massive roof trusses for the church may have been sourced in one of the earl's protected forests but we don't know which one.

The medieval economic landscape and place-names[13]

The close relationship between the landscape and the economic activities of the medieval population (both Gaelic and English speaking) enables us to drill down further into the appearance of the countryside in the absence of any written descriptions. For instance the presence of sheep rearing in the early medieval period is evinced by the Gaelic place-name *Auchmuty* (G. *áth multin*) signifying the crossing place or ford of the castrated rams, and by *Walkmill* indicating the fulling of cloth. *Bowhouse* on the high ground above Brunton relates to the keeping of cattle as does *Byresloan* on the lower land where dairy cattle would have been reared. The name *Sauch Park* near the modern day railway station indicates a low lying boggy place where willows

---

[11] *St Andrews Liber* 420-421

[12] Brunton Charter 1685. NAS GD26/3/950

[13] Source : PNF II

grow, important in basket-making. Nearby *Brooms and Broomfield* suggest another important economic resource used for thatching.

As regards evidence for the existence of a church at Markinch we have only the single place name Pittenhaggles (*G. Pett an eaglais*) Gaelic for *the share of the church* and an old disused mine known as the *Glebe Pit*. Perhaps the Gaelic place-name *Fettykyl* (G. *fiodh cill*) referring to the *wooden church* of nearby Leslie hints that the contemporary church at Markinch was made of stone but it could equally have been made of oak beams or mud and wattle, such is our ignorance of pre-12th century Scottish building practice.

Chapter 2

2. Evidence of an 11th century building

An early link with Lady MacBeth?

Written Evidence

It is rare in Scotland to have ecclesiastical charter evidence from as early as the 11th century, but in Markinch we do have such proof from the days of Bishop Maoldhùin (Maldunus) of St Andrews (c1028-55). It is recorded that Maoldhùin, Scotland's premier bishop, granted the church with all its land to the monks of Loch Leven Priory.[1] It is one of the earliest such references in Scotland and deserves special mention as it was a grant taking place at a time when MacBeth was on the Scottish throne. At around the same time, MacBeth and Gruoch his wife granted to the priory monks of Loch Leven possession of Kirkness near Portmoak and Bogie near Kirkcaldy. It might reasonably be asked whether there was any link between the two generous acts of piety, that of the King and Queen on the one hand and that of the King's premier bishop on the other. Fiona Watson has answered this by suggesting that Bishop Maoldhùin of St Andrews joined with MacBeth and Gruoch in donating the church and its land to ensure that masses were held for the eternal souls of the King's party should they not return from a well-attested pilgrimage to Rome[2]. Clearly great store was placed upon the power of prayer emanating from this ancient institution. The pilgrimage party is likely to have comprised a mixture of secular and ecclesiastical representatives. If, as is now generally accepted, Gruoch was a member of the MacDuff family[3] then the choice of Markinch may indicate a link between MacDuff kinsmen and the local church even at this early period. The church may even have stood on or adjacent to Gruoch's own land.

---

[1] Liber cartarum prioratus Sancti Andree in Scotia, The Bannatyne Club 1841 - referred to hereafter as St Andrews Liber. (p. 116)

[2] Watson, F. (2010) MacBeth, a True Story. Quercus

[3] Woolf, Alex 2007 From Pictland to Alba, p 247 (a theme developed by Taylor, S in PNF V)

The written evidence tells us that there was a church at Markinch in the 11th century but we need to investigate more closely where it was located. Stylistically it could not be the same building as the one represented by the tower still standing today. It is likely to have been a more primitive structure, whether of timber or of stone, but where was it located?

Topographical evidence

The landscape that we explored in the previous chapter might give us a clue to the likely location of an early church. Standing beside the eastern apse-like structure on the side of the present day church looking east, if we were to strip away the modern houses and the railway line, flood the drained land of the Glebe and the Myres, we would find that we were looking out over a long stretch of water. To our left would be a stream (the Markinch or Back Burn) flowing into the loch and to our right at the bottom of the mound would be a well[4]. It must once have been a strikingly beautiful place and whether it was selected by the first Neolithic settlers or by the early Christian missionaries it had much to commend it as a place of devotion. This is especially true given the importance of water to early belief systems. All over eastern Scotland we find ancient sites with these characteristics. As for alternative locations, there is no other site in the Markinch area that matches this one in terms of the characteristics we would associate with an early place of worship. The 11th century church and probably several places of worship before it were almost certainly located on the hill where the church now stands, most probably close to the east end of the mound where the later chancel was built.

Radar and Resistivity Analysis

In year one of the project, Dr Oliver O'Grady undertook a radar survey of the church interior. Conditions were not ideal and, apart from the barriers created by fixed pews above floor level, there were significant obstacles below the church floor including stone beam supports and heating pipes. Fortunately, 19th century drawings collected during the early survey stage of the project enabled us to identify most of the sub-floor features and these were taken account of in the final analysis. A more serious obstacle was the air gap between the floor and the ground surface underneath. This made readings particularly difficult. In addition, limited resources meant that only

---

[4] known until recently as the Juck's Waal

a single horizontal slice was taken by the equipment. Nevertheless, the results confirmed the robbed-out foundations that enabled the outline of the Romanesque church to be confirmed[5].

However, no clear image was obtained of any earlier church building. If the topographical argument for the siting of the early church is accepted then this can only mean one of two things. Either it indicates that such a structure was based upon the same foundations as the later chancel or that the slender foundations were disturbed beyond recognition when the bodies lying under the church were taken away in the post-Reformation period. It could also, of course, be a result of the radar's lack of accuracy due particularly to the air pocket under the floor.

It was decided to examine the ground outside the church as aerial photographs had revealed a semi-circular feature curving around the south and east sides of the church. This resembled the kind of ditch and bank

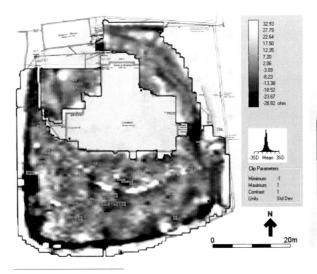

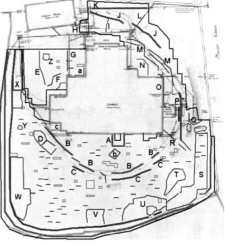

5 O'Grady, Dr Oliver. (2013)

feature often found enclosing a medieval churchyard. Preliminary sounding with a metal implement indicated that there were still slabs from an earlier path along this line and this was going to make interpretation difficult. Had the path been laid on top of an earlier feature or did the path represent the feature itself?

A complete resistivity analysis of the graveyard was carried out. After careful scrutiny of all the features marked by letters on the second diagram as well as a study of historic drainage plans, the following conclusions were reached.

The resistivity readings pick out the line of a former path, shown clearly in 19th century plans and tested with probes. It shows up as a white curvilineal feature to the south of the church in the first diagram and as the interrupted line marked B on the second diagram. However, the meter was unable to penetrate the stone or concrete surface and no clear evidence of an underlying ditch could be determined along the line of the hollow followed by the path.

The raised "bank" to the south of the path shows up with a darker shading in the first diagram and is marked C on the second diagram. The archaeological report referred to several possible interpretations including *"a foundation trench, perhaps for a path, an enclosure wall, or a small ditch."* (O'Grady 2013).

Feature J is referred to as *"a prominent curvilineal low resistance anomaly, at the north and north eastern side of the graveyard"* (O'Grady 2013). It runs along the top edge of the northern slope of the churchyard, interrupted in the middle by the path. The archaeological report notes *"The interpretation was not clear but it may be the remains of a robbed-out enclosure wall or small ditch, or an unrecorded large drain though this is perhaps less likely."* (O'Grady 2013)

The anomalies marked M, shown as parallel high resistance (red) and low resistance (blue) lines on the plan are interpreted as path and drain respectively except the most easterly section of low resistance. This *"may be representative of an earlier feature. The location and alignment may suggest that this could be more closely associated with anomaly J and may be the remains of a robbed out wall, section of a small ditch or unrecorded drain."*

Anomaly P next to the boiler house is likely to pick up a number of superimposed features including modern drains. The report concludes that *"it is unclear whether earlier archaeological remains are recorded here, but it is feasible that part of the readings may relate to the extension of the feature identified by anomaly J and potentially a section of robbed out wall."*

Despite the references to possible walls and ditches, it was clear from this preliminary resistivity analysis that modern features, particularly the path laid in the 19th century, were largely obscuring any earlier features that may remain.

It was therefore decided to use radar to take a series of sections across the curvilineal "hollow and bank" features referred to in the previous section. As anticipated, the ground penetrating radar was able to pick up features underlying the path that did not show up on the resistivity plots. The report is cautious in referring to these underlying features as *"either foundations for the path or the remains of a ditch on which the path has been built"* (anomaly 50, O'Grady 2013). It seems unlikely that a path designed for light traffic would have foundations that go down to a depth of around 0.8m and so a ditch is the most likely interpretation (although a ditch inside a wall is unusual). The raised ridge-like feature running in parallel and to the south of the hollow is described in the technical report as *"perhaps the foundations of a wall or a bank with a stone core."* The same features are picked up in several of the other cross sections.

With reference to the curvilineal feature, the report concludes :- *"The earthwork feature seems likely to have a recent paved path in the depression on the south side of the graveyard, supported by the high resistance readings and radar anomalies along its apparently fragmented length. However, the resistance data also showed a low resistance response along the south side of the earthwork and extending into the north east of the graveyard, which might be a small ditch or a robbed out wall. The radar data also suggested the existence of a cut feature under the path, possibly a foundation trench or truncated boundary ditch. Supporting the resistance data the radar also suggested the possible existence of a truncated wall feature or bank along the south side of the path. This boundary feature could be ancient in derivation and would be in keeping with the kind of circular or pear-shaped walls or enclosures that surrounded Scottish churches with medieval or early medieval origins. Such enclosures need not have a monastic association, but are generally indicative of a medieval burial ground."* (O'Grady 2013).

If this feature is to be interpreted as a burial ground enclosure associated with the church that preceded the 12th century one then it would most likely have been on a fairly small scale to allow room for both church and burial ground within the same enclosure. Clearly, more archaeological work, including excavation, is required to clarify the position.

Other evidence

There are two stone bowls, probably piscinae for washing sacred vessels, embedded in the church yard wall. These seem to have been found during the 1920s when houses were cleared away at the bottom of the kirk hill. They appear to be roughly finished and not of the high quality that we would associate with the 12th century church. They may date back to an earlier building and provide further evidence for its location on the hill.

On the church building itself, early survey work identified two long rectangular stones that have been reused as lintels above the south eastern door. They appear to be the remains of a simple triangular arch of the kind found in several Anglo-Saxon churches in England[6] although we should

---

[6] eg St Andrew, Brigstock and St Peter, Barton-upon-Humber

be cautious with this evidence as there are examples as at Dunfermline where such triangular arches represent a conservative element in an otherwise Norman-style building. They could therefore give us clues either to the appearance of the 12th century or the 11th century building.

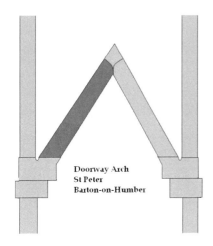

Doorway Arch
St Peter
Barton-on-Humber

Recent research has been unable to locate a stone unearthed under the church in 1884/85 that may one day provide more proof of the site's early Christian or even pre-Christian origins. It was described as a stone "three feet wide, a foot thick and six feet long". It was made from a huge slab of fetid limestone. According to a writer of the time "it bore some rude sculptures, and had a hole in the centre".[7]

The radar picked up two locations, both towards the east of the church that could relate to such a stone, assuming that it was left in situ. An easterly location is also indicated by the architectural drawings of the period which show a proposal to dig a service trench under the church leading west from the boiler house following the wall-line of the former chancel.

None of the pieces of evidence reviewed in this section when taken on their own are sufficient to prove that the 11th century church was once located under the eastern portion of the modern building. Taken together, however, the combined evidence is compelling and we should not look beyond the walls of the existing building to seek the site of the ancient church of Markinch.

The end of the old church

Given the number of years that it took to build a church in the 12th century, we would expect the pastoral needs of the people to be taken care of during the construction phase. When a church was being replaced this would mean that the old building remained standing whilst construction took place on perhaps an adjacent site. On an extensive site such as Durham this difficulty could be overcome by building close to the original Saxon church, or as at Dunfermline by building over and around it. On more restricted sites

---

[7] Derek Hunter (1984) quotes this but does not give sources. It was probably from a newspaper article of the time.

such as the one at Markinch it is possible that the 12th century building rose as an annex to the older 11th century structure, albeit as an annex that dwarfed the original structure. It may even have been necessary to build up the site with imported material to ensure a flat site close to the original building. At Bonkle in Berwickshire a pre-Norman apse is still attached to a later chancel arch despite the loss of the rest of the building. At Dalmeny, A. J. Turner[8] found that the various elements of the church were built in stages to ensure continuity of worship. Larger buildings that have been excavated such as Dunfermline Abbey Church show that there were often strong religious reasons to build one church as an annex to another or on top of another. In Dunfermline's case a well a few yards away from the old church indicates the possibility of a pre-Christian place of devotion.

The appearance of the 11th century church

As for what the old pre-Norman church looked like we have nothing to

guide us in the absence of firm archaeological evidence. There were probably several churches on the site and the one that is referred to in the mid 11th century text could well have been made of stone, perhaps a smaller version of the two chamber church unearthed at Dunfermline under the existing church or a building similar to the lower stages of Restenneth tower. As already noted, it may be significant that a neighbouring church in Leslie was known as Fettykil or "the wooden church", perhaps in contrast to a near neighbour built of stone. As discussed later, the old church could have served as a chancel while the new one was built and this is shown in the illustration along with an imaginative reconstruction of the now lost stone found in the 19th century.

In England there is a wider range of Saxon period examples of stone churches still standing, but whether they can be compared to contemporary buildings in Scotland is

[8] A. J. Turner, 1948. Dalmeny Masons' Marks. Treatise framed in Dalmeny Church

open to debate. The 10th and 11th centuries were probably times of experimentation and fusion of styles but we should not think that Scotland was cut off from continental influences. Ideas relating to building and design could be derived from pilgrimages to Canterbury or Rome and of course transmitted on vellum between ecclesiastical centres. Of course if the builder had sufficient power and resources there is no reason why they could not simply import an entire construction team including the master mason.

It is more than likely that a church close to a seat of judgement in the heart of the MacDuff landholdings would have been in many ways special. When the MacDuffs were returned to power under Malcolm and Margaret, their prestige was restored and they were given a position at the apex of the Scottish nobility with unique privileges in terms of law, leadership in battle and even the right of crowning the monarch[9]. This would have accorded them the resources to ensure a striking and permanent monument at Markinch[10] but might the church have been built by a bishop or a prior? The following chapters turn to this 12th century building which fortunately leaves us a few more physical clues as to its general appearance as well as written evidence regarding its changing ownership.

Further Investigation of the pre-Norman remains

Outside the church, an excavated cross section of what may be a ditch would help clarify whether the remains of a former elliptical cemetery belonging to the 11th century church can be identified. Within the church, it may be some time before the opportunity arises to excavate under the floor boards but it is suggested that the east end of the building would be most productive. One clear target has been identified under the former chancel arch. This may be the decorated stone

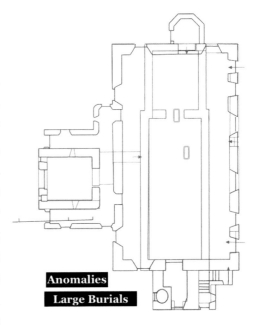

Anomalies
Large Burials

---

9 see the writings of Hector Boece, John of Fordun and Andrew of Wynton

10 Manson, B. Fife. 2012 Why a Kingdom?

unearthed in the 1880s or it may be an important burial. Either way it is believed that its identification will throw light upon the church mentioned in the mid 11th century charter or possibly one of its predecessor buildings. External excavation close to the eastern gable wall under the existing foundations might also identify stratified bone material capable of being dated.

3. The Romanesque Tower

Survey Results

This chapter begins to describe the tower from the ground floor up. The removal of modern plaster from the interior ground floor walls during 2014 enabled the tower to be better understood in a number of significant ways discussed later. The chapter focusses upon what we can see remaining above ground, while the following chapter concentrates upon a reconstruction of the lost elements of the building.

Despite its remarkable state of preservation there are many features that have been removed from the tower, particularly the woodwork and that almost certainly includes the spire. Some decorative features are also missing and we would not expect the building in its original state to have been as austere as it now presents itself, although perhaps its relative lack of ornamentation may have protected it from further destruction during the Reformation. Since that time it has had a number of functions and has probably been in continuous use since it was built, a feature relatively rare in Scotland for a twelfth century building.

Also rare is the quality of the stonework indicating a high level of sophistication on the part of the master mason and high level of discipline and skill amongst the workforce. The debate is ongoing on the original function of the building and the likely balance between the religious and secular activities for which it was designed. Impacting upon that discussion is the possible identity of the builder, which is further discussed in chapter 7.

A stone tower would have been essential to preserve from fire those objects precious to the church such as relics and manuscript books. Increasingly during the 12th century the secular authorities used written charters and other records and they would also have required a safe place for storage. As is argued later, the tower would have had both sets of functions and may even have been intended as a place of refuge in time of war. This mix of the spiritual and the practical was addressed in a papal edict of 1123 which forbad the fortifying of ecclesiastical buildings[11]. There are examples after that date of fortified churches along the coast of France but we should not ignore the advances made in defensive buildings throughout Britain and Ireland when examining towers attached to buildings with a primarily religious function. Markinch tower has all the hallmarks of a good quality castle, rapidly built and to a high standard. Such castles spread northwards across England and into Wales from the time of the Norman Conquest.

External features of the tower

Foundations

The first thing to note is that the foundations were discovered to be very shallow in the 1920s when they were surveyed before underpinning with concrete[12]. This contrasts with St Rule's which has substantial foundations. The tower at Markinch appears to have tilted to the south during the early stages of construction. Rather than starting again the builders seem to have simply compensated for the tilt by increasing slightly the thickness of the ashlar blocks on some of the lower courses. If the same masons had moved on from St Rule's to Markinch, as is sometimes argued, it is unlikely that such a mistake would have been made. The minor subsidence may also

---

[11]First Lateran Council, Canon 14, Medieval Sourcebook, Fordham University

[12] Hunter, D. (1984) p 20

indicate that the ground was made up from transported sand as has already been suggested.

Plinth

Measured around the chamfered base course from north to south, the base of the tower measures 5.03m (16' 6"). Measured from east to west, 1.05m of the tower is clasped by the nave and it projects 4.2m from it, making a total of 5.25m (17' 3"). Research in the field of medieval measurement is not conclusive but as far as we can determine 16' 6" was a frequently used length for the standard rod during the 12th century. We should also be cautious as scales were most likely variable from one region to another during that

century.[13]

The chamfered plinth sits upon a square base. The form of the chamfer is similar to St Rule's but contrasts with the much smaller building on St Serf's Inch, Loch Leven which has a square plinth. The plinths at Dunning and Muthil are ill-defined but the latter appears to have a chamfer. The closest parallels to the shape of the tower plinth at Markinch are the early 12th century plinths at Weaverthorpe and Garton-on-the-Wolds in Yorkshire but even a great building such as Durham with foundations laid down just prior to 1100 has a similar style of chamfer but on a grander scale.

It might be noted that at Markinch the first course of stone blocks above the chamfered plinth is thicker than all the others. This may be to provide a strong base or it may be aesthetic. It could also indicate the importance of different parts of the building. At Markinch the lowest course of the tower

[13] Zupko, R. E. 1977. British Weights & Measures: A History From Antiquity to the Seventeenth Century. He notes that in the late 13th century a law known as the "Composition of Yards and Perches" fixed the rod at sixteen and a half feet representing the former fifteen German feet used previously by both Anglo-Saxons and Anglo-Normans.

and nave is 39.4cm (15.5") in height, slightly more than the courses above it which vary from 30.5cm (12") to 35.6cm (14"). What is thought to be the east chancel wall, on the other hand, has a lower course fully 44.5cm (17.5") in height, surmounted by a second course that measures 41.9cm (16.5"). This was perhaps considered by the masons to be the most important element of the building justifying an extra large set of base stones, despite its smaller size as a building element.

The masons had a tendency to use sandstone blocks with a quartz vein running through them on the exterior of the building whereas this stone is less frequently used inside. It may have been thought to be more resistant to weather. There is a wide variety of sandstone types represented on the building. This may represent the complexity of local geology but suggests that the blocks came from a number of quarries in the vicinity. The mortar used on Markinch tower has so far not been analysed. Limestone seems to have once been extracted locally and the name "Limepotts" appears in one charter.[14] The lower courses at Markinch have more blocks that are cube-shaped or higher than they are wide, whilst the upper courses are more elongated. It is not clear whether this is an aesthetic choice, a change in building practice or perhaps even an attempt to give the tower a greater apparent height through visual effect.

The thickness of the wall at the base is 1.2m (3' 11") considerably thicker than it is on the second floor. Whether this was primarily for defence or to support the weight of the superstructure is difficult to say but if the tower had a defensive function then we would not expect it to have any doors on the ground floor. The western arch also would have been an obvious weak point allowing access to anyone entering the nave and so we would expect not only a stout door but also high, small and defensible windows on the nave and chancel, perhaps accompanied by a clerestory gallery accessible through the first floor door between the tower and the nave.

The lowest course on the north side is less weathered than elsewhere, probably due to the fact that the ground under the small door had been built up at some point in history, burying the first course but making the second course more susceptible to weathering, particularly frost damage, being at ground level. This gives the stones the impression of being older. The earth

---

[14] 1797 Sasines no. 4950 Quoted in PNF II (Inchinnie)

was removed in the 1880s and a ladder (now removed) was installed restoring the northern doorway to its original position several feet from ground level. A single faintly visible mason's mark was revealed. It matches one further up the tower on the inside, possibly indicating that base and tower construction took place within a relatively short space of time.

An early 19th century poet[15] expressed fears that the tower might one day collapse and the 17th/18th century extension to the south may have included an element of buttressing, visible from inside the loft The foundations were found to be relatively shallow during a Ministry of Works survey in 1929 and concrete underpinning was inserted.

A west facing door?

We do not yet know whether the insertion of the late 18th century door in the west wall of the tower obliterated a former door or not. If defence was an important factor in the tower's construction then it seems that such a door was unlikely. To take two early 12th century examples from Scotland and Yorkshire, neither Dunning nor Weaverthorpe had a western door. The illustration without a door by Alexander Galletly in the late Victorian period may

---

[15] Taylor, Robert. 1811

have drawn upon some local knowledge[16] of the 18th century renovations. If there was a door in the 12th century then the truncated aperture above the existing door may have been a spy-hole as well as a light source. The church's main door is likely to have been in the nave and south facing in an analogous position to the blocked archway on the existing south wall. A grand western entrance was an imported mid Georgian fashion that within a few years probably led to the blocking of the tower's arch when the force of westerly winds was realised. Initially this would have been provided with an inner door but eventually the arch was blocked permanently with rubble, providing a support for the new balcony. As discussed elsewhere we now know that the small elevated north door on the tower was a later insert.

Overall building quality

The most striking feature of Markinch church tower is the regularity of the stonework and the harmonious proportions of the four segments of the building separated by the string courses. There are 9 to 11 stones of very similar size between the longer quoins on each course. Clearly, standardisation and quality control were of a very high order. A modular construction method is also suggested by the fact that the distance between the first and second string course equates to the width of the building (16' 6", one rod). All the courses appear to be original 12th century except the topmost two courses which from their size and markings are 19th century. Compared to St Rule's there are remarkably few instances where a course diminishes or increases in height as the masons worked their way around the tower. There are two courses that are slightly narrower for no apparent reason and it may be that these are topping-off courses using cap stones put in to protect work at the end of the season and provide a base for the following year.

putlog holes

The putlog or scaffolding holes were re-opened in the 19th century and do not appear on early illustrations. They oppose each other internally on all sides of the tower and are deep enough to have allowed a double set of cross

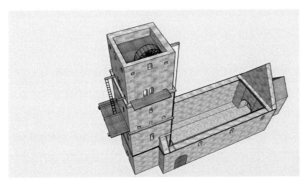

beams at right angles to each other to have passed right through the tower. These would have projected externally providing a strong, cantilevered structure around all four faces of the tower and a solid internal base that could have supported

the weight of a crane. The angles of the chafing around the east facing slots indicate that they may have supported inward facing struts supporting a higher platform or a jib.

The string courses

Two separate rows of diamond or lozenge patterned string-course stretch around the tower (and probably once adorned the nave exterior as well). They are badly eroded except on a small section of the south east corner of the tower where the shape of the lower face is clear. No evidence was found to support Walker's

reconstruction of these features showing a triple row of lozenges[17] and it is most likely that there was only one row, or at the most two (one on the face and the other on the chamfer). Decorated friezes are found on the exterior of high status buildings such as La Trinité in Normandy, Peterborough and Durham Cathedrals from the late 11th century through into the early 12th, although their use on lower status early 12th century towers such as that at St Nicholas Twywell was not uncommon. Cormac's Chapel, Tipperary provides us with an Irish example from 1124-1134, and they seem to have become more fashionable later in the 12th century, particularly in Scotland where they are a prominent feature of both Leuchars and Dalmeny churches. At Markinch they mark the first three interior floor levels, the second string course being neatly integrated with a finial on the apex of the 12th century roof. As a way of dating a building their use seems more to depend upon the status of the building itself, the resources of the builder and the background of the master mason. Their use need not therefore suggest a mid or late 12th century construction date but could indicate a high status early 12th century date.

The diamond or lozenge motif can be seen on several 12th century buildings in Scotland[18] which suggests it may have had some kind of particular significance, perhaps among the native clergy, as the design pattern does not seem to be prominent in buildings associated with imported monastic orders. Perhaps the diamond or lozenge motif had more of a symbolic than a decorative function[19], and a single diamond frames a motif on Brechin tower below and opposite the crucified Christ. The motif is also occasionally used as a simple design element in some English parish churches. An example with a double row diamond motif from early in the century can be found in the interior of the small early 12th century church of St Nicholas in Risby in Suffolk but this is used internally rather than externally. At Markinch the string course may represent the coming together of native symbolism and Anglo-Norman taste as at Cormac's Chapel in Ireland. Whatever Markinch's string-courses may or may not say about the dating of the building they certainly give the tower a unique appearance. The

---

[17] Walker, J. Russell. 1895. *Pre-Reformation Church Architecture in Fifeshire*

[18] This includes Dunblane, Muthill and St Margaret's Chapel..

[19] Richardson, Hilary. *Themes in Eriugena Writings in Early Irish Art* in Dunne, M., McEvoy J. J. (eds) History and Eschatology in John Scotus Eriugena and His Time.

choice of design was most likely that of the patron on the advice of the Prior of Loch Leven. If painted when new their effect would have been even more immediate but so far external painting has not been demonstrated on buildings of this period.

Belfry Openings

The openings on the tower at Markinch are unusual and appear to be windows rather than simple sound holes. Two small single-stone arches with a plain grooved decoration are supported by three columns with cushion capitals with simple lunettes. The flanking shafts and capitals are engaged, that is they are not free standing but cut from the same stone as the window surround. The bases that the column stands on are slightly bulbous. What is unusual is that most 12th century belfry openings are framed by an exterior arch, whereas at Markinch the

arch is on the inside. Twin bell openings not set under a containing arch are usually a pre-Norman feature[20] but in Markinch's case the stonework clearly points to an Anglo-Norman influence.

In addition, the stone supported by the middle column does not pass from one side of the wall to other as at St Rule's and many other 11th and early 12th century towers. Whether this is a sign of innovation, sophistication or a late development of a commonly used window model depends very much upon when the tower was built. Another possible explanation is that they were based upon a domestic or castle model rather than an ecclesiastical model. The openings have some similarities with St Rule's and some differences which are discussed later. The groove running around the small

[20] eg St Andrew, Bishopsone, Sussex. See also Fernie, E. 1999

40

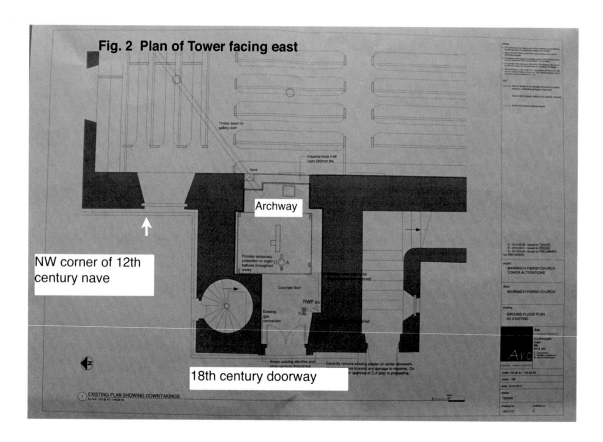

Fig. 2 Plan of Tower facing east

Archway

NW corner of 12th century nave

18th century doorway

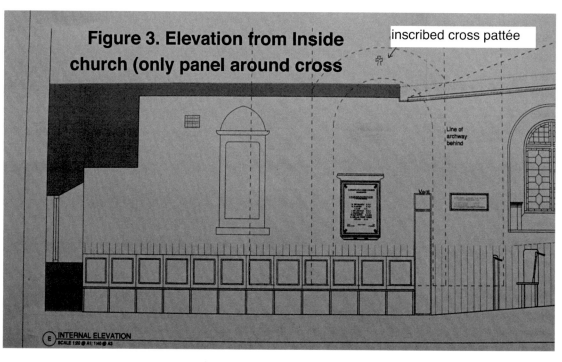

Figure 3. Elevation from Inside church (only panel around cross

inscribed cross pattée

Line of archway behind

single-stone arches may be particularly significant as it is one of the elements shared with St Rules and is part of the architectural repertoire of some early Norman designs from Caen in Normandy (see page 98). These very high status royal buildings used elaborately carved foliate rather than cushion capitals but their overall design influence was widespread. It is, of course, possible that the patron specified this window form to reflect the design of the old building demolished to make way for the new.

Interior features of the tower

Spiral stair access

The steps and the newel post sections of the stair have been cut from the same block of stone. The steps themselves have been pared back to allow access to rooms but it is not clear whether these cutaways (see photo) are original features. Although a rope is now used there is evidence from socket holes that a handrail was once in place at least at lower levels. The arching above the stairs is constructed from rubble, probably held in place until set by a wooden scaffolding as with the lower portions of the tower stairs at Cormac's Chapel and Durham Cathedral. As with so much of the building we must remember that timber is gone and only the stone remains. The stair may have continued up as far as the spire within a wooden framework. A single piece of *in situ* timber remains at the top of the steps, but it is not clear whether this is 12th century or later.

During 2014, the cement and plaster wall-covering was carefully removed from the ground floor following an assessment of the lower layers of plaster which turned out to be 19th century. This revealed a previously unrecorded entrance to the tower stair. A massive lintel above the door giving access to the stair seems to have cracked, probably when the western door was inserted in the 1780s. This may have necessitated the blocking up of the door

to support the lintel. As noted on page 23, a new access door may then have been inserted on the north face of the tower. It would then have been at ground level due to the accumulation of debris around the tower. The monolithic arch above the small door gives the impression of antiquity and its elevated position has been thought of as defensive and compared to Abernethy and Brechin towers[21], indicating a Gaelic influence. We now know that such comparisons are no longer valid and the ground floor of the tower probably presented blind faces on all sides being accessed only from within through the internal tower arch and up the spiral staircase.

Traces of a wheel winch?

The plaster removal also revealed two rectangular sockets opposing each other on the north and south walls. The top of each slot is 1m 98cm from the existing floor level. Both slots are 15cm wide but the socket on the northern wall is slightly higher (30cm) than the socket on the southern wall (22cm) indicating that they may have held a transverse beam secured temporarily with a wedge. The depth of the sockets was not ascertained as they had been backfilled with lime mortar. The hypothesis is put forward that the sockets may have contained the spindle for a temporary wheel winch used to lift heavy weights up the tower during construction. A peg hole and set of cut marks on the wall, possibly associated with a rope, are visible next to the socket on the southern wall. Such a device with a radius up to 2m could probably lift several tons powered by one or

[21] Semple, M-C. 2012

Fig. 1 Suggested position of crane winch

two men walking inside the wheel. We have to be cautious in interpreting these slots but the use of such a machine could underscore the importance of the building and the status of its patron.

The diagram shows a cutaway of the ground floor of the tower looking north with the newly uncovered stair doorway and lintel on the left.

Stonemasons' marks

These were fully surveyed under the supervision of Moira Greig MIfA and are considered more fully in chapter 6 but the following features were observed on the ground floor. Over 800 marks were identified on the tower, mostly inside although some were on the external wall facing into the nave. The majority on the ground floor are simple two or three stroke banker marks most probably applied for identification and payment purposes. Two stand out as perhaps indicating a higher status of mason. The first is in the form of a roman numeral five or a V-shape with three cross-strokes or serifs, making five chisel marks in total. The second is an hour-glass or bow-tie shape of four stokes. After several trial attempts this mason appears to settle for a mark where the last stroke of his diagonal surface dressing constitutes the first stroke of his mark. He thus clearly "fingerprints" his stones and his work can be identified all the way up the tower. As Moira Greig points out, however, the picture is probably complicated by apprentices occasionally marking the stones of their masters. Examination of the spiral staircase

Instruction on half-bonding technique

revealed that there was some specialisation, with specific marks being applied to the difficult curved stones.

The most remarkable stone on the ground floor is about sixteen courses from the present day ground level. It has been marked with the bow-tie sign but also includes a diagrammatic representation of the very accurate half-bonding technique that is such a feature of Markinch tower. For whatever reason one of the senior masons appears to be clearly depicting on stone for all to see how a strong and elegant structure should be put together. Half-bonding is a technique that is also used at St Rule's and Dunfermline but is much less strictly adhered to on comparable towers at Dunning and Muthil. The photograph with the purple marking shows how it was applied in practice giving Markinch tower its distinctive appearance.

A survey of stonemasons' marks elsewhere in the east of Scotland was carried out as a postscript to the project.[22] Other 12th century buildings in

eastern Scotland such as Leuchars and Dalmeny have some overlap with the marks at Markinch. For instance the roman numeral five or V-shape is to be found at Leuchars but generally each church has a distinctive clustering of marks. The marks at Dalmeny are more complex than those at either Markinch or Leuchars, many of them with serifs adorning letters of the alphabet. Only two commonly used marks are shared between Markinch and Dalmeny compared with four shared between Markinch and Leuchars and as many as six shared between Leuchars and Dalmeny. Markinch has a higher proportion of simple two and three stroke marks than the other two. Legerwood in Berwickshire was also surveyed. It has a distinctive grouping of marks but again with significant overlap, particularly with respect to simple arrows, asterisks and crosses. The samples from Dunfermline, Birnie and Bonkle were interesting but too small to be significant. One double arrow mark at Markinch (illustrated) was identified by Moira Greig as being unique

22 Manson, B. 2015. Stonemasons' Working Practices A Comparison of 12th Century Churches in the East of Scotland

in a Scottish context but recorded in Germany. Most can be found elsewhere in one form or another down through the centuries. Few marks were found at Tyninghame, Abernethy, St Rule's, Dunblane, Muthil or Dunning, raising questions about different methods of payment or the use of dyes as markers.

Marks are an important part of a building's story. Nevertheless, there is always the temptation to read too much into the phenomenon. Although most are likely to have been associated with payment practices some also seem to relate to quality and status within the work team. They are in effect the only visible and enduring manifestations of a range of complex working practices that we will never fully understand. They have, however, been largely overlooked in the literature, perhaps because of the fear that the modern rational observer has of association with some of the wilder theories of the past. It is perhaps time that a balanced approach is taken to this fascinating heritage, particularly with respect to the 12th century. The Markinch data and the comparative material collected following the survey should provide a firm basis for further study. Chapter 6 provides a deeper analysis for those who wish to take the study further.

Tower arch

Compared with many arches throughout the country, Markinch tower arch is remarkably simple in form. It has a double set of voussoir stones, one built on top of the other rather than being stepped back. The tower side of the arch has been opened up as part of the project but most of the nave side is still under 19th century plaster. It will be interesting to see whether the other side of the arch is more decorated than the side that has been revealed.

The height of soffit or underside above existing ground level within the tower is 3.91m plus a further drop of 0.4m to the floor of the present day church on the other side making an overall internal

The tower arch from above (west facing side)

height of 4.31m (14' 2"). Its internal width measures 2.01m (6' 7") and it has a depth (wall thickness) of 1.07m (3' 6"). Its dimensions and simplicity make it comparable to many early Romanesque towers but until further investigation of the nave side is carried out it will not be possible to tell whether it is genuinely early or a throwback feature on a later building.

There are two orders or rows of voussoirs (arch segments) all of a regular shape and remarkably similar in size. Only those at the crown of the arch deviate from the standard thickness and this would be because these were last to be inserted on top of the wooden frame that supported them during construction. About half have masons' marks on the face but there are no marks on the underside of the arch which is constructed of well tooled ashlar of a very high quality. A section of panelling was removed on the nave side of the arch revealing an incised "cross pattée" on the topmost stone. This is dealt with more fully in the chapter covering the nave.

Tower Arch - Piers and Imposts

It is usual for Romanesque arches to have a decorated frieze on top of the column and just under the point where the arch begins. It may once have supported the wooden structure underpinning the arch whilst it was being constructed but at some point it became a conventional adornment. The decoration on this impost block often returned along the wall in a form similar to a string course or dado rail.

Shaved impost and shadow profile

At Markinch this feature was found to have been removed at some time in the past, the rough surface having been chiselled away and plastered over as can be seen in the photograph. Fortunately a "shadow" was left on the wall at right hand side of the arch outlining where they were once positioned. This shows that they would have measured 22cm in height and projected 5cm from the arch with a simple profile, the lower chamfer 50 degrees from the horizontal. It seems more likely that they were removed for religious or aesthetic than for practical reasons unless clearance was required later for a large door filling the entire arch. Unfortunately it was not possible to access those parts of the pier where any hinge sockets would have been located but a door of this dimension seems unlikely. Neither has it yet been possible to reveal any impost decoration on the nave side of the piers.

Both upright piers were plain ashlar but there are indications that plinth facings at the bottom had been removed in a manner similar to the imposts. A square socket, an elongated slot and one nail were noted, both on the south pier although about one third of the depth of the arch is still concealed with brickwork and rubble on the side closest to the former nave where an 18th century door, slightly narrower than the arch, was likely to have been located.

If the tower did not originally have a western door then it begs the question as to why the tower arch was so high. Was it simply an architectural convention or was there a liturgical purpose, either to frame a particularly sacred area on the ground floor of the tower as seen from the nave or perhaps to provide a grand entrance for the occasional procession of relics kept in the upper stages of the tower?

First floor & access from the tower to the nave roof space or balcony

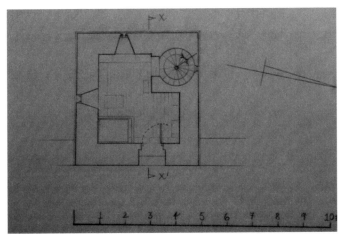

This room is entered from the stair to the south through a narrow slot or passageway cut in the steps. It now houses the disused sand pit for the weights formerly used as part of the clock mechanism. The entrance doorway from the stairs is original and integral to the

Doorway leading to arch above nave

construction of the tower walls. It has two sets of sockets that would once have held door hangers.

The first floor room gave access to the upper levels of the nave through a massively linteled door shown in the photograph. When the walls and ceiling of the church were raised in the 19th century the entrance was partially blocked and it was necessary to insert a couple of wooden steps to gain access to the loft space at its new level. The side of the doorway facing the nave was framed by a voussoir arch (see following chapter). The sockets here seem to relate to a solid door frame but these may have been later inserts when the tower was used as a prison.

The room is well lit having windows facing west and south, larger than those in the floor above. The insides of the windows are splayed and arched unlike those at St Rule's that have straight through tunnel-like windows. The first floor walls are thinner than those on the ground floor evidenced by a step or ledge at floor level without any special surface dressing. The floor may originally have rested on this step and been slightly higher than it now is. Currently the room is 5.18m high (17 feet) corresponding closely to the external string courses. If any kind of ceremony or display took place on a balcony overlooking the nave then this would have been the preparation room[23]. If instead the door led to a strongroom or arms store above the nave then this could have been a guardroom. The room could even have been a small private chapel analogous to the room suggested by Fernie at St Mary's Deerhurst[24].

Second floor

The doorway from the stairway to this room enters to the east, that is towards the church, rather than to the south as was the case with the level

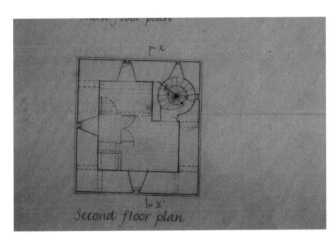

below. This time there are two steps that lead down to the floor, assuming that it is at its original height. Several steps on the stair next to this room have been replaced using red sandstone. The wall to the left of the opening has been re-patched, possibly to remove some devotional item that had originally been built into the wall face. The windows in this room are smaller than those below but equally well executed with a small monolithic (single-stone) arch on the outside splaying inwards to a voussoir arch on the inside.

The room now houses the clock mechanism and is 11 ft 4 ins (3.4m) in height. There are six putlog holes at floor level.

Third floor - belfry stage

The room is 2.59m (8 ft 6") in height although it is possible that the ceiling is from a later period given that the beams cut into two of the arched windows to support the 19th century bell-frame. Without this apparatus the height of the room would be 4.95m (16'3'), comparable to the first floor.

[23] Semple 2009 suggest a ceremonial display of relics from a balcony accessed through this door

[24] see Fernie, E. The Church of St Magnus Egilsay in Crawford, B. (ed) 1988

As noted above, at Markinch the insides of the belfry windows are carefully finished with single inward-facing arches. The display is as much to the inside as it is to the outside. At Dunblane, Muthill and Dunning the arch is on the outside. This may indicate that the "belfry

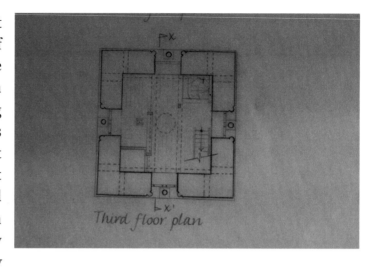

Third floor plan

room" at Markinch was envisaged originally as a habitable place such as a summer scriptorium or observation room rather than a bell chamber, and the windows would certainly fit well into a domestic style building. Few domestic buildings from this period survive and so the Markinch windows are a rare example of this combination of architectural forms. Although the tower itself is relatively simple, the master mason may have expressed his inventiveness though his design of the belfry windows, perhaps showing evidence of his experience with domestic or defensive structures.

As far as we know there were no resident monks at Markinch that had to be called for prayer from the fields. The insides of the belfry windows at Markinch have square slots that could have supported an interior shutter frame but no signs of the sloping grooves for wooden slats that would have deflected the sound of a large fixed bell downwards, as is the case at St Rule's (although slats could have been inserted into the shutters). The parishioners in a small town such as Kirkton of Markinch could have been summoned to mass by a handbell such as the one still kept in Birnie church in Moray. It is more than likely, at least in summer, that the generous

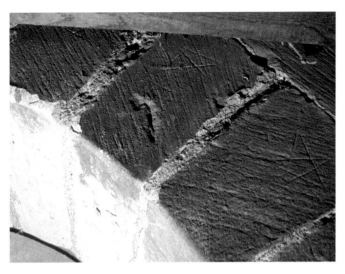

windows at Markinch let in light to a room where records could be read and copied or important visitors given a bird's eye view of the Shire. Shutters, closed individually from the inside, would have sealed the tower from the prevailing wind in summer and from storms in winter when candles and cressets could have been used. We have little knowledge about the use of window glass at this period.

The mason's mark on almost all the voussoirs is the five-pointed star, again an indication of some degree of specialisation amongst the stonemasons.

Top floor

This floor now has a 19th century domed ceiling constructed of packed stone that has later been concreted, perhaps to consolidate the tower against the downward pressure of the stone spire. The tower is likely to have had a timber spire in the 12th century but no traces remain. The squat pyramidical

spire replaced with a stone spire in 1807 was most probably a replacement much lower than the original. Measured to the top of the last course of masonry showing a 12th century masons' mark, the room's height is 2.36m (7'9").

The room has four squat windows that would have

provided an excellent view of the surrounding countryside. There is an oval niche on the north wall which Semple (2010) interprets as the possible remains of a reliquary safe box found in a similar position on other Scottish towers.

It is also worth remarking upon two interesting examples of graffiti on the top floor. The first is a deeply carved cross accompanied by the initials AP. The A has a v-shaped cross-bar. Given the confidence of its line it may well be a dedication cross but the initials are puzzling. An attempt at an

Grafitti interpreted as beam crane and roof trusses

interpretation is given in chapter 7 along with a photograph. The second appears to be a rough drawing of a T-shaped crane, complete with counterweight at one end and rope hanging from the other. Next to it are what appear to be roof trusses in various stages of assembly.

Construction

How long did the tower take to build?

It was clearly a major undertaking for its time. Building is very much a seasonal activity and mortar requires frost free conditions to set. Records show that cathedrals took decades to construct with many changes in design along the way. However, the evidence at Markinch suggests that the tower at least was constructed fairly quickly. This should not surprise us given the historical context of many defensive stone towers being built all over the British Isles in the hundred years following the Norman invasion. The status of the MacDuff family and their command of resources is also a significant factor to consider. Skilled masons and wrights could be paid for and unskilled labour recruited either under kinship or feudal obligation.

The stonemasons' marks indicate that it was essentially the same core team of masons that began and finished the project, most likely overseen by the same master mason. Some specialists were drafted in for particular tasks, such as the stair well and the voussoirs around the windows at the belfry stage.

The first storey, including the tower arch, may well have been completed within a year. The wall around this stage is much thicker than the walls further up the tower and for whatever reason, structural, defensive or financial, the decision may have been taken after year one to build a lighter structure. It is likely that internal scaffolding rested upon this ledge as there is no sign of any putlog holes at this level although external scaffolding may have been used as well. The wheel winch could have been raised onto a platform at this level, before moving up the tower as the building progressed.

Two new sets of masons' marks make their appearance on the first floor (asterisk and arrowed slash). One of these continues on to the second floor and the other does not. On the very top course of the second floor the five pointed star makes an appearance and continues to be prolific at belfry level and on to the upper floor. This appearance of the star internally corresponds to a clear change in block size when viewed externally. It looks like a new building season, most probably the third, started a couple of courses below the belfry string course.

An aerial drone was used to take detailed images of the stonework. The putlog holes indicate that the entire platform was taken down and reassembled, both externally and internally, as the building progressed. Additional lighter scaffolding would have ensure that the upper courses that were being worked upon remained at roughly chest height. Work continued on the belfry stage in year three but the wall appears to have been capped by a thinner course three or four courses from the top of the tower. The following season, putlog holes show that this layer was used as a foundation for another platform. The fact that it was so close to the top indicates that the construction of a wooden spire was a considerable undertaking involving its own scaffolding frame.

The evidence so far assembled points to a short four or five year building campaign for the tower rather than a period close to a decade that was the initial hypothesis. Quarry prospecting, ground preparation and foundation digging may have added several years to the project depending upon how much of the hill had to be augmented with transported material. As noted in chapter 1, the nearest sand quarry, not rendered inaccessible by south facing

fertile farm land, was the north side of Markinch Hill where long terraces may represent sand quarries set up for lines of ox carts circumnavigating the hill, dumping material on the church site and then returning (see photo

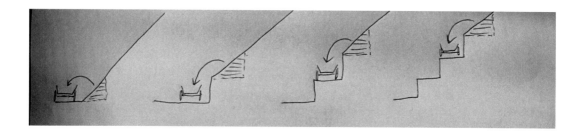

above and diagram below). There are, however, alternative explanations for these terraces although none is satisfactory.

The nearest stone quarry was at Northhall although another one may have been opened at Sythrum to the south close to the Leven where quartz-veined sandstone was to be found. These transportation activities would have involved substantial wagons drawn by teams of oxen and the builder would have drawn upon a workforce that was predominantly local. An additional year or two could well be added if there was a significant amount of lime washing and painting. Although the chancel of a church was normally first to be built, the situation on a restricted site such as Markinch may have meant using the existing church as the chancel and as a consequence the new chancel may well have been constructed last in the building sequence or perhaps years later if the former church was left *in situ*. The best estimate for the overall project, based upon existing evidence and a number of assumptions would be around a decade from start to finish.

Archaeology and Conservation of the Tower

Following full architectural and photographic surveys of the tower interior, a team of conservation masons carefully removed a layer of 19th/20th century plaster and cement that covered the 12th century ashlar up to a height of 2.6m. A rotting timber ceiling dating from the 19th century was also removed opening to view the double voussoir arch that would once have linked the tower and the nave. The arch was blocked and partly damaged as a result of 19th century works to the church interior. The working organ bellows were left in situ but it is hoped that in future they can be replaced by a more compact set giving us a clear view of the arch.

The cement skim that covered the wall dated from the 19th and 20th centuries. The graffiti were carefully photographed before removal but the oldest was 1942 lending weight to the 1930s dating when the foundations of the tower were consolidated. No underlying plaster was discovered except around the lintel of a small door that once led to the spiral stair. It was left *in situ*. Red paint covered the ashlar and the surface of wooden pegs that would once have held panelling believed to have been 19th century as it also once covered the raw wall interior on either side of the door cut in the 1780s. Where moisture was present in the underlying ashlar, removal was relatively straightforward. However, tight bonding to a dry base meant that great care had to be exercised to preserve the 12th century ashlar surface in certain areas. Eventually it was decided either to remove only the top layer of cement by gentle chipping or to leave the entire covering in patches to represent part of the building's history.

The timber ceiling turned out to be much more decayed than had been anticipated. It was photographed before removal for safety reasons. Some dry rot was detected in the back panelling which was partly removed. The rest of the panelling was left in place as it contained deafening material designed to shield the congregation from the noise of the bellows. The joist removal revealed that the imposts of the arch had been chiselled away but a profile was obtained in the form of a shadow impression on the south wall.

A laser scan was part of the survey work carried out by the former R C A H M S .[25] A quinquennial review of the building is also carried out by the Church of Scotland. It is clear from the current condition of the tower that it will require conservation within the next few years. Some settlement and water penetration require

urgent attention and the necessary works will open up the opportunity to examine areas that were inaccessible to the current research project.

This includes the east side of the tower arch, particularly the lower section from the imposts down enabling the entire arch to be compared to others such as the east arch at St Rules. A small sample of timber from the top of the spiral stair could also provide useful dating evidence as could further charcoal samples taken from inside the rubble of the lower walls where the

[25] now part of Historic Environment Scotland

18th century door was cut. Initial samples of what was probably hazel proved to be unsuitable for Carbon 14 analysis but lessons for future work have been learned in discussion with profession archaeologists.[26]

---

[26] Thanks to Mike Cressey of CFA Archaeology for useful advice on screening and sampling

Chapter 4

4. The Lost Romanesque Church

Reconstructing the plan, profile and interior of the 12th century nave and chancel

At Dalmeny, near South Queensferry, we find a well preserved nave and chancel but a lost tower. At Markinch it is the reverse with a tower that has lost most of its nave and chancel. We cannot, however, simply assume that Markinch's nave and chancel looked like those at Dalmeny or that Dalmeny's lost tower resembled the tower at Markinch. Firstly, there was great variability between building projects in the 12th century with a variety of patrons and master masons all with their own knowledge of churches and cathedrals elsewhere and their own motivations for building. Secondly, we do not yet know how many years separated the two projects. Similar parallels might have been sought with Leuchars but sadly both nave and any tower that might have existed are gone and the remaining apse is designed with a semi-circular shape at the eastern end. At both Muthil and Dunning both nave and chancel seem to be later than the tower and at Dunblane the original tower is believed to have been free standing[1].

Markinch lost its nave and chancel by stages and more detail is given in chapters 8 and 9. In brief, some time during the 17th or early 18th century there was a major reconstruction of the church. The south facing walls of the old church, both nave and chancel, were knocked down and the wall that we see today was constructed up to the level of the tooled stonework comprising the topmost courses of the wall (this was part of a later heightening). This project enlarged the building by moving the wall south by a few metres. We can see from the choice of quoin stones that it was the intention to lime-wash the building and there was no attempt to conceal some fairly shoddy stonework. Squared and tooled stones from the old building were torn down

---

[1] Fawcett, R. Corpus of Scottish Medieval Churches (accessed July 2016)

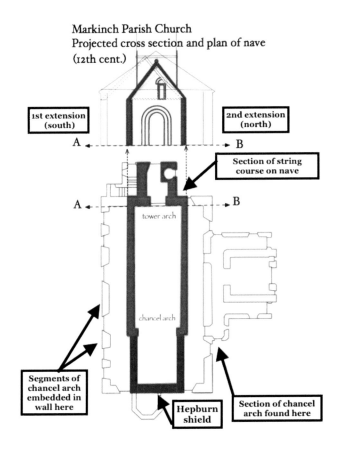

Markinch Parish Church
Projected cross section and plan of nave
(12th cent.)

1st extension
(south)

2nd extension
(north)

A

B

Section of string
course on nave

A

B

tower arch

chancel arch

Segments of
chancel arch
embedded in
wall here

Hepburn
shield

Section of chancel
arch found here

and reassembled along with rougher material straight from the quarry. Since that time some of the windows have been widened but the general appearance of the main facade today is similar to what it once was in the days of the reformers. The reconstruction allowed the pulpit to be placed in the middle of the church and the focus moved around 90 degrees from the old chancel.

At the back of the church, on the north side, some of the old Romanesque walling must have remained and it was not until the early 19th century that a further enlargement took place, this time moving the wall a similar distance to the north. This was associated with the heightening referred to above. As the sketch shows (not to scale) these two major enlargements almost destroyed the 12th century nave and chancel and it is only in recent years that their very existence has been demonstrated through the current research project. What now remains and can we attempt to reconstruct the outline of the original Romanesque structure?

the west gable wall of the nave

Only a few fragments are still to be seen of the actual nave. These are the gable ends attached to the tower, and two cusps of stone that would once have protected the nave roof show that the tower and nave were built together as part of a single structure. The section of remaining nave wall to the north of the tower has been damaged by the insertion of a window in the late 19th century and the piece to the south of the tower has been almost enveloped by the staircase giving access to the Balfour loft.

Enough of the northerly section of nave gable remains to show that the plinth was identical to that of the tower, although some of the corner stone is partly hidden underground within the burial area. As part of the project, some 20th century cement was carefully removed from the edge of the corner stone. This was enough to demonstrate that it butted up against a later piece of red sandstone, presumably part of the 19th century foundations for the northerly church expansion. It showed that the corner of the nave was a mere 1.27m (4' 2") from the tower. Assuming that the nave was symmetrical about the tower this gives us a total width of (5.03m+1.27m+1.27m = 7.57m) or 24' 10",

one and a half times the width of the tower. The unit of 16.5 ft or 5.13m (one rod/perch) is also a key element in the construction of two late 11th century cathedrals (Ely and Tewkesbury), indicating that the measurement was used from an early date as suggested by Eric Fernie[2].

The west gable also has a small section of string-course

line of 12th century nave wall

[2] Fernie, Eric. (1999) The Architecture of Norman England

remaining strongly suggesting that it once stretched in a continuous band around both tower and nave (we have no evidence for the chancel). We can pick it up again on the same gable on the southern side of the tower, although in a much worn state. This suggests that the nave did not have the type of projecting corbels that are a feature of St Rule's, Leuchars and Dalmeny.

Roofline raggle marks

The inside surface of the original west wall has been well preserved and can be studied from inside the roof space of the present day church building. The deep grooves aline with successive roofs butting up against the tower and can be clearly seen. These are the lines where mortar and lead ensured a waterproof join between the tower and the nave. Three separate post-12th century roofs have been identified and it is this analysis that has enabled the progressive enlargement of the church to be fully understood as outlined in the introductory paragraphs.

However, with respect to the 12th century Romanesque building, the steeply pitched roof line stands out from the rest. The line is surmounted by the ghost image of a long-lost finial. The roof pitch is 50 degrees to the horizontal and can be traced via two capstones, one inside the church and the other outside, to a point just above the decorated string course on the outside (NW corner). Early on in the survey, an exercise in geometry provided us with a theoretical location for the north west corner of the nave, which at that time was buried within cement. The calculations placed it 1.17m (3' 9") from the north wall of the tower which is within 0.076m (3") of the figure that was eventually measured empirically once the cement had been removed. It is a technique which could usefully be used with other medieval buildings elsewhere in the country.

The east wall of the chancel

Towards the centre of the eastern gable our early observations noted a section of wall with ashlar blocks similar to those on the tower. Indeed, the lower courses are even larger, contrasting with later rubble stonework to the south and with broached (grooved) ashlar to the north. There is a clear junction with later walling indicated by a corner stone and several quoins above, still visible despite the tie stones that are later inserts. This corner stone does not line up with the north western corner of the nave referred to in the previous section and it is proposed that it is the north eastern corner of a chancel slightly narrower than the nave. Parallel lines projected towards each other from these "corner stone points" are about 0.46m (1' 6") apart.

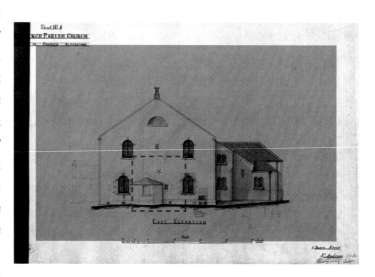

The image shows the the Hepburn Shield (red) and the position of a window (green) superimposed upon a 19th century drawing. It is believed that both were inserted into the wall at a later date when improvements were carried out to the chancel. The 12th century gable wall is outlined in blue but it would originally have risen to an apex before the roof was piended (hipped) in the 17th century as shown in a contemporary drawing. A section below ground is shown by the blue line

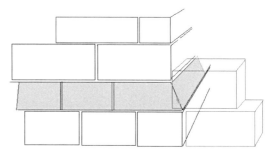

as the ground level is considerably higher now than it was in the 12th century.

The corresponding south eastern corner stone of the chancel is not visible, perhaps hidden within the masonry of the more recently constructed boiler house. However, looking up, several well aligned quoin stones can be made out above the southern wall of the boiler house defining the south-eastern corner of the chancel. The chancel appears to have measured 6.4m (21') in width as compared to the estimated nave width of 7.6m (25'). Such a slight difference in width between nave and chancel is by no means unusual for the period and can be observed at Dunning[3].

Also hidden are the lower stages of the plinth and it is recommended that these be excavated to determine whether it is significantly different from the exposed nave plinth to indicate a different building date. It may be that the two are contemporary and that a deep plinth course simply served to emphasise the importance of the chancel or compensate for a drop in ground level.

Ground Penetrating Radar Results

During 2013 these measurements were tested using ground penetrating radar under the floor of the church building. They were plotted upon the more detailed RCAHMS measurements that became available earlier in the year. The analysis was able to eliminate 19th century features such as service channels and sleeper walls supporting the floor due to the availability of highly

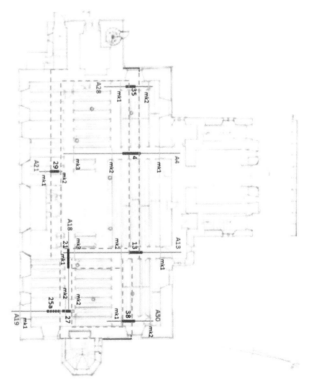

3 Warwick Rodwell (2012) notes that the inside line of the the nave wall was often projected to provide the outside line of the chancel wall.

accurate late 19th century architectural drawings.

Lack of space, time and resources meant that the radar survey was confined to the collection of simple raw reflection data along a series of two dimensional transects. These were restricted to accessible walk-ways by the fixed furniture within the church. Moreover, ground slope and in particular the air gap between floor and ground level made interpretation complicated. Nevertheless, the ground conditions were otherwise favourable, and experienced interpretation combined with the availability of plans showing existing sub-floor features meant that meaningful results could be obtained.[4]

The cross sectional profiles produced by the radar picked up evidence of the north and south wall foundations at five separate points under the present day church showing a separate nave and chancel. Generally these measurements confirmed the external observations, although further confirmatory work is recommended particularly in relation to the south wall where a modern service duct has obscured some of the radar readings. Radar also appears to have picked up a substantial burial between nave and chancel and this enables us to produce a reasonable footprint of the original 12th century building. This matches well with the analysis of the raggle lines on the tower and their projection down to the tops of the original walls.

The initial interpretation from the radar results suggested that the medieval wall of the church was less than 1m wide and with the remains extending to a depth of c1.2-1.6m.

Was the chancel built at the same time as the nave?

It might be noted that although the ashlar on the middle portion of the east wall is of a high quality and very similar to that on the tower, the chamfer on the plinth appears to be slightly different. Additionally, there is also a stone plaque with John Hepburn's coat of arms on it towards the top of this section of walling. Hepburn was Prior of St Andrews Priory in the early 1500s and it has been argued that he was responsible for rebuilding the chancel, perhaps re-using stones cut in the 12th century.[5]

---

[4] full details in O'Grady. 2013

[5] Corpus of Scottish Medieval Churches, St Andrews University (accessed April 2016)

The question here is whether the shield marks the date of this piece of walling or whether is it a later insert. If the chancel is a rebuild using original ashlar blocks then they have been very expertly dis-assembled and re-assembled. It would have made no sense in terms of liturgical layout to have widened the original chancel but we may entertain the possibility that it was lengthened by Prior Hepburn necessitating a new set of foundations to the east of the original founds. Of course no trace is left of the north and south walls of the old chancel to test this hypothesis. However it may be noted that no radar trace was picked up of a robbed foundation trench to the west of the existing wall, suggesting that the wall is either original or sitting on original foundations.

It is more likely that Hepburn inserted the shield following improvements he carried out to the 12th century chancel These may have included the addition of a central east facing window, the sill of which is to be seen immediately above the shield. The most suitable place for such a shield on the gable wall might

Hepburn shield with canopy reset in wall at St Leonard's

have been immediately below the window, necessitating the removal of several stones from the top of the 12th century wall. Hepburn inserted his coat of arms into several ancient buildings including St Rules, St Leonards Chapel as well as the north wall and the gateway of St Andrews Cathedral.[6] This was probably connected to his bid to be elected archbishop of St Andrews (unratified by the Pope).[7] It is suggested here that the shield was a later insert into the existing chancel wall, completed at a time when Hepburn was carrying out improvements to the building.

---

[6] For images of these see saint-andrews.info "the shields of St Andrews"

[7] Dictionary of National Biography No 26

The central position of the shield on the modern day wall indicates that it was not inserted after the church had been expanded to the south. Neither does it line up well with the post-Reformation door into the church that is to be seen inside the boiler house which is central to the gable as it would have existed post expansion. This suggests that it was inserted by Hepburn himself rather that as a recycled artefact.

It is also worth noting that the plaque is raw edged and does not have the elaborate stone frame associated with some of the other examples of Hepburn's shield. However, above the shield are the remains a small projecting canopy that may have been chiselled off when it was intended to lime wash the building in the 17th or 18th century. Such a projecting canopy is a feature of several of the shields in St Andrews. The plaque may have been left in place at that time as it was intended to cover it up along with the rest of the walls.

Finally, returning to the chamfered plinth stones themselves, they are badly worn but would not be out of place underpinning the wall of many 12th century churches in Yorkshire or Northumberland. What we are seeing is probably only the top of the plinth, the rest being buried under accumulated earth. This can be concluded from the fact that the floor of the boiler house is somewhat lower than modern day ground level and that the arrow sharpening marks are some 43 cm (17") lower than shoulder level. Bowmen would have had to bend down to sharpen their arrows if the ground had always been at its existing level.

There is another reason for the 12th century builders changing the type of plinth at the chancel end of the church and that is simply that the east end of the site is lower than the west end and a slightly elevated plinth would have been required to keep the chancel level with the nave.

We are therefore left with two possibilities. One scenario is that the chancel was built at the same time as the rest of the building and the larger plinth stones represent the relative importance of this part of the church and the lower level of the land at this end of the hill. Alternatively the chancel may have been built slightly later than the nave when the entire building came under the control of St Andrews Priory some time after 1166/67 or even after 1240. One reason for this might have been that the old church was not demolished until the entire building and its revenues passed into the hands of the Priory *"in proprios usus"* during the 13th century. It is apparent that Hepburn did not build the chancel, partly for the reasons referred to above and partly because he had no motive, family or otherwise, for a major rebuilding project in a place such as Markinch. In fact he most probably drained the revenue pertaining to Markinch church for projects closer to home such as St Leonard's College where a plaque is also to be found similar to one found at several other St Andrews sites.

More recent stonework is visible above the 12th century ashlar blocks for several courses and this is likely to relate to the first expansion south in the 17th century. This enlargement would have meant the demolition of the southern chancel wall. Any window at the east end would have been blocked as a loft for tradesmen was installed beneath a hipped or piended roof (as shown in an 18th century sketch). The slightly raised eaves line can still be seen level with the top of the south wall prior to its being raised. Higher masonry, marked with a distinctive pecked tooling, would have been added when the church was further widened and heightened in the early 19th century.

The east wall is in fact a complex structure that will require closer analysis when it is repointed. On balance, the central portion is probably 12th or 13th century with substantial later alterations above and to either side. Two doors (both now blocked) have been pierced in the east gable at different times. Inside the boiler house is what is probably a post-Reformation three-centred flattened arch that was blocked in the late 19th century. Further towards the north east corner of the church is a simple blocked doorway that would have given access to an under-stairs storage space in the 18th or 19th century. Both doors are visible marked with faint red dotted lines on the drawings of 1884[8].

Overall Dimensions

As expected, both nave and chancel appear from the radar results to be symmetrical to the tower. The building would therefore originally have had three separate elements with the following external dimensions :-

[8] Gillespie (1884)

	Width (N-S)	Length (E-W)	Height (eaves)	Height (apex)
Tower	5.03m (16'6")	5.25m (17'3")	22.25m (73')	N/A
Nave	7.6m (25')	16m (52'6")(est)	6.1m (20')	10m (32'10")
Chancel	6.4m (21')	7.5m (24'7")(est)	4.88m (16')	8.69m (28'6")(est)

The junction between nave and chancel has not been precisely determined by the radar and the above estimates are based upon radar indication of what is taken to be a chancel burial. The nave may have been slightly longer and the chancel correspondingly shorter. The estimate of the height of the chancel is based upon the assumption that the roof had the same 80 degree apex with a 50 degree pitch as the raggle marks of the nave etched out on the tower would suggest. No estimate has been attempted for the top of the spire on the tower due to lack of evidence. The above table therefore represents the best estimates that can be arrived at given the few actual measurements that we have. It will be important to cross-check these when the full architectural survey is complete. They do demonstrate, however, how much can still be discovered about Scottish churches that were significantly damaged during periods of Reformation destruction and 19th century reconstruction.

The arch linking the nave and chancel

The dimensions in the table above had been established by the end of year 2 of the project but an extraordinary find at the beginning of year 3 added

considerably to our ability to reconstruct the interior. Within a once railed off area to the north east of the church, once owned by the Balfour family, a stone was overturned which was recognisable from its design as having been carved in the 11th or 12th century. It was outside the building but within a few feet of where we would expect a chancel arch to have been located inside. It turned out to be a hood moulding (projecting outer order) from an arch[9] of some considerable size. The stone was curved, having a bead or quirk on the inner arc and a saltire motif on the outer arc. This design was relatively common throughout Europe from about 1070, probably being based upon a wooden chip-carving tradition. Its earliest appearance in curved form on an arch voussoir seems to have been at L'Eglise de la Trinité de Caen in Normandy between 1070 and 1100. From here it spread rapidly throughout the British Isles[10], gradually diminishing in popularity throughout the 12th century as more exotic chevron designs became more fashionable. The two designs, however, overlapped for many years making both difficult to use in terms of dating.

When the hood-moulding was found, the stonemasons were on site working on the removal of plaster within the tower. They worked with the volunteer team to measure the diameter of the original arch using a template

[9] Thanks are due to Richard Fawcett for confirmation that this find was part of a hood-moulding

[10] Baylé, Maylis 1979

and a simple piece of string. This method has its limitations but the best estimate finally arrived at was 4.9-5.1m (16-17ft) which accorded well with our earlier estimate of 7.6m (25ft) external nave width. It was enough to conclude that the outer arc of the arch between the nave and the chancel stretched between the north and south walls with some space for a short stretch of wall on either side. What we had found was a segment of the arch that must have been left embedded in the northern wall of the church when the entire southern wall (and with it most of the arch) was demolished in the 17th/18th century. When the church was widened for a second time in the early 19th century the demolition team, perhaps with the encouragement of the Balfour family, had set aside a reminder of the old kirk. It was placed within the railings (now gone) of the family cemetery for safe keeping along with a fragment of a tombstone also displaced from the building. This must have happened around 1807 when major works were undertaken and Lieutenant-General Robert Balfour, known for his antiquarian interests, was head of the family.

It soon became apparent that the curved section matched three similar sections that had been built into the south wall of the church some time in

the 17th century following demolition and rebuilding. Several plainly tooled voussoir stones are also visible in the same wall and may have come from the same arch. They are, however, difficult to identify with certainty and will have to be examined closely and measured when pointing is next carried out.

An arch of this width would probably require a double row of voussoirs underneath the hood moulding to have the necessary stability and we can make an attempt at reconstruction based upon the simplest arch of this period at Birnie in Morayshire. However, given the status and resources of the MacDuff family and their close links to the Scottish monarchy we need not confine ourselves to comparators from within Scotland. They would most likely have been

familiar with some of the most sophisticated building within England, both those drawing upon an Anglo-Saxon tradition and those drawing upon new technologies and design ideas from Norman imports.

A hint that the chancel arch may not have had the simplicity of Birnie is given by a preserved engaged foliate capital re-used within the 19th century Session House next to the church. It appears to be surmounted by an inverted pillar base and has suffered much from erosion over the past half century. An early photograph shows it to have been an elaborately carved feature that may well have once underpinned the arch. Sadly, there is insufficient detail either in the old photographs or on what remains today of the capital to provide an estimate of date. As with the segment of chancel arch referred to above it is possible that the capital was rescued from the north side of the nave or chancel when church widening took place in the early 19th century.

The Upper Door Linking the Tower and the Nave

The small door accessing the nave roof space could have had a number of functions. It could simply have given loft access for storage purposes or access

Arched door looking down into nave

to a clerestory balcony that went around the upper stages of the nave. An alternative function was explored by Mairie-Claire Semple who saw it as giving access to a display area where relics were shown to the congregation below on feast days.[11] It could even have led to a domestic "croft" or living quarters as at Cashel. The arch is certainly well designed with a neat set of voussoirs looking as though it was designed to be seen rather than hidden away in an attic. It contrasts with the simple lintel used on the tower side of the door.

Whether the upper arched door led to a balcony or a storeroom, we have to account for why it is offset to one side unlike St Rule's and several early English churches where the upper doorway is centrally located. This could relate to the architecture of the roof timbers and may indicate that central king posts were used. These would have obstructed any central door access to the higher levels of the nave[12]. At St Rule's two slots on the east tower wall indicate that the original roof timbers of the nave were supported in a different way.

The nave side of the tower arch

Recent building archaeology work uncovered the side of the arch facing into the tower and a substantial part of the soffit. As already noted all the imposts and friezes on this side had been removed with a chisel. It was not possible to access the other (nave) side of the arch except at the very top where

[11] Semple, M-C. 2009

[12] Thanks are due to Neil Sutherland for this insight.

wooden panels were removed. The upper voussoir stones were of plain ashlar with a prominent cross inscribed on the topmost stone. The cross was cut within a set of still visible rectangular guidelines. Its simplicity indicates that it was perhaps cut by a senior mason as a dedication linked to the building process rather than as an ornamental part of the nave's overall decoration.

The cross may have been once covered in plaster as traces of a white material were present in the cut grooves. If this were the case then the actual nave could have been decorated in paint upon plaster according to the designs of the patron. If so, then the cross would have been completely hidden under the plaster, its existence known only to the masons. However, more comparative work is required to find other inscribed crosses in similar locations. Other explanations could be advanced, including the possibility that it is a later dedication or re-dedication mark.

Windows, roof structure and covering

We have absolutely no physical clues as to the form of the 12th century windows in the nave and chancel. If security was important to the builders then they are likely to have been relatively small and set high up in the nave walls. Dalmeny gives us an idea of what could be achieved later in the century but as no finds of chevron decorated stone have turned up at Markinch we might expect something much simpler, closer to the appearance of the windows found in the tower. A supposedly 12th century window with angled voussoirs on the inside, rubble fill and a small single stone arch on the outside survives at St Martin in East Lothian and, although, less skilfully executed than the work on Markinch tower, may give some idea of the nave windows, especially if Markinch was originally designed with security in mind.

As with the windows there is virtually no evidence left to give us an idea of what the roof structure looked like. A roof with a king post could be open or closed, with or without a flat ceiling. Was there an open framework of beams increasing the lofty aspect of the narrow nave or was there a ceiling at eaves height, possibly with a room or attic above? Was there a display balcony in front of the small first floor door between the tower and the nave or did the door give access to a clerestory or even a loft-space. The answer will only come through careful analysis of similar buildings elsewhere in the country.

Some evidence exists as to the material that covered the roof at one point in its history. When the southern walls of the medieval building were demolished in the 18th century slabs of brown mudstone were used to pack the building stones reused on the new wall. These can still be seen in a number of places. During the work on the tower a small piece of this mudstone was retrieved from the packing under the arch. It appeared to be broken off across a pierced hole but more samples will be required to verify this. No other waterproof material has been observed and unless the original building had wooden shingles later replaced with mudstone then the conclusion drawn is that the 12th century building was covered in mudstone slabs.

The overall appearance of the 12th century building.

In assessing the overall impact of the church to the eye, we turn away from the reasoned deductions based upon physical evidence that have characterised the previous paragraphs. We have been able to reconstruct the shell of a building from those pieces that were untouched by the ravages of the Reformation and zeal of the 19th century church improvers. We now have to rely upon evidence from elsewhere in the country, upon assumptions, upon analogies and to a degree upon imagination.

As chapter 7 seeks to demonstrate, all of the men, whether lay or ecclesiastical, that had anything to do with the construction of the 12th century building are likely to have occupied the highest ranks of the Scottish aristocracy and we would expect any building constructed to have been something out of the ordinary despite the lack of carved stonework so far found.

With this combination of social position and resources we should not confine ourselves to Scotland or even to the North of England when we are seeking comparators for Markinch church. Skilled labour and design ideas could have come from sources throughout Britain. Indeed we know that the elite travelled widely, whether on pilgrimage to Rome or on Crusade to lands further afield.

Despite the likely involvement of wealthy patrons, the tower arch in particular is remarkably simple in design for a building of such sophistication. Only the upper voussoirs of the tower arch have been inspected on both sides but they reveal a lack of carved ornamentation on the stonework. This could be explained by the fact that it was a deliberate reflection of a similarly shaped arch on an earlier building. It could, however, have been that it was lime-washed and elaborately painted along with the rest of the nave and chancel. It could of course be that the church is earlier than we have previously thought.

The tower when built would have been visible from miles around and, like the tower of St Rule's, may have served as a marker beacon for pilgrims. Markinch was certainly on one of the principal routes that would have been taken by pilgrims travelling from Dunfermline to St Andrews. We have no remaining evidence, but colour may well have been used externally, particularly on the now lost south facing doorway. A particularly striking feature may have been the bands of lozenges around the tower and nave. Might they also have been painted when the tower was new? It is believed by archaeologists that Pictish stonework was painted without lime-render, and colour may have been used in a similar way by the Gaels.

Once inside the building, the pilgrim's eye would only gradually have become accustomed to the light. Even in summer there were probably dark corners lit by cressets or candles. What is much more difficult to recreate is what a visitor would have seen painted upon the walls. It is quite possible that a significant proportion of the expenditure lavished on the church went, not upon stonework, but upon brightly coloured paintings and designs that are now long gone or upon items of ecclesiastical furniture. They would not have been simple decoration but would have told vivid stories intended to impress aspects of morality on the minds of commoners and noblemen alike. A single fragment remains from 12th century Glasgow Cathedral, and the paintings on the crypt of Canterbury Cathedral are well known. Recent work at the early 12th century chapel at Cashel has revealed the richly painted decoration on the plastered walls and ceiling.

Future Archaeology

A relatively simple excavation at the east end of the building should give us important information about the plinth arrangement and foundations of the former chancel. Burial material below the foundation may, as at Dunning, increase our knowledge of the pre-12th century church. Any future opportunity to examine under the floor of the church should concentrate upon the east end and in particular under the chancel arch where a major anomaly was recorded by radar. As regards future archaeological research on the fabric of the church building, it is possible that traces of wall paintings still exist hidden under Georgian lath and plaster or post-Reformation whitewash. Any remaining traces of paint on the nave walls would of course be confined to the interior of the west gable and any on the chancel would be on the inside of the east gable. Non-destructive archaeology of a church always leaves the prospect of something else for future generations to discover.

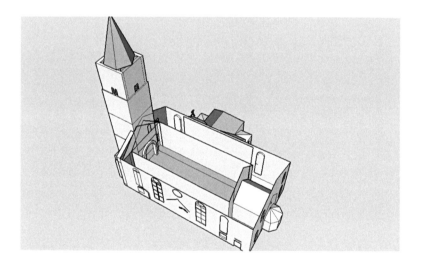

Chapter 5

5. Some Comparisons with Other Romanesque Buildings

It is not only the Scottish climate that has resulted in the country's poorly preserved building heritage. Buildings were systematically defaced at the time of the Reformation and this may have been the fate of the imposts and freize linked to Markinch's great tower arch. There seems to have been an attempt to strip buildings of all forms of decoration, and this attitude towards a building's past continued well into the 19th century with the result that there are very few examples of original ornamentation left in Scotland compared to other European countries. Those vestiges that do remain from the 12th century are gathered up in this chapter and compared to the features described at Markinch in the previous two chapters.

The review begins with Markinch church's east of Scotland neighbours and then moves further afield on the assumption that churches in Scotland may have drawn their influences from a wide hinterland. It is important to note at the outset that, apart from the cathedrals, few of the ecclesiastical buildings from the 12th century are securely dated to the satisfaction of all historians or art historians. We are therefore comparing the vestiges of Markinch church with other vestiges built over a wide timespan and drawing upon a wide range of skills, influences and resources. Crudely constructed buildings can often be confused with "early" buildings and conversely a high quality building in Scotland need not necessarily be "late". A recent study of Yorkshire[1] which has many 12th century churches still standing concludes that the quality of workmanship varied enormously making it virtually impossible to arrive at even approximate dates by visual inspection alone. The history and the archaeology of a building are both essential and, even with good evidence on all fronts, there will be continuing debates between experts.

Against this background, the chapter confines itself to observations rather than detailed analysis and complex arguments around dating, although

[1] Wood, R. (2012) Romanesque Yorkshire. Y. A. S. Occasional Paper No. 9

where dating is secure through written evidence it is provided. Also provided are dating estimates by reliable authorities although given the above caveats we need to seek out and experiment with more reliable methods.

11th-12th Century Churches in Eastern Scotland
St Serf's Inch, Loch Leven

St Serf's chapel, like Markinch tower, is constructed with squarely cut ashlar blocks but its scale and function as a building is very different. If the building had a western tower accessed though one of the two vestigial arches, then this no longer exists. The building blocks were presumably ferried or sledged to the island during a winter when the loch was frozen. Much of the building has been damaged or reconstructed but the north facing wall suggest that the structure belongs to a different building tradition from Markinch. There may have been an attempt to lay the stones in a pattern formation rather than in regular similarly sized blocks. Two broad stripes of stone blocks, most higher than they are wide, stretch across the north face of the building with two narrower courses sandwiched in between and an elongated course below. This contrasts with the attempts at regularity of course height at

Markinch. The plinth that the building sits on is square with a chamfered course above. This is similar to Markinch tower and nave where the chamfered course is much deeper, perhaps reflecting the greater scale of the building. Vestiges of arches can be seen on the east and west walls.

Restenneth

Again we find the use of patterned stonework, particularly in the lower and presumably older courses of the tower. That, alongside the use of ashlar blocks set vertically on edge points to building techniques from an earlier era, although it is clear that the tower has been rebuilt and renovated several times. Worth noting, however, is the simplicity of the tower arch (believed by most to be original), the small door above it and the triangular headed windows on each face of the tower. Markinch displays classic Anglo-Norman building techniques but the tower arch appears from

what we know to have had a fairly simple unadorned appearance. Two reused lintels at Markinch may indicate a former door with a triangular arch, again pointing to a pre-Norman aesthetic incorporated into an essentially Anglo-Norman style building (but note the use of this arch technique over windows at Dunfermline). No masons' marks were found at Restenneth and it is likely that, as a monastery, it would have used a high proportion of relatively inexperienced monks in the building process compared to the highly skilled and most probably imported labour that is evident at Markinch. The upper part of

Restenneth tower appears to be later than the lower part and has some finely cut ashlar blocks but these are not aligned in strictly half-bonded fashion as at Markinch and the cutting back of stones surrounding the small tower windows indicates that the tower, at least in its later form, may have been lime-rendered. It is difficult to imagine external lime-rendering at Markinch given the precision of the facing ashlar.

Restenneth points to the difficulty of using the quality of building techniques as a guide to dating a structure. A well-resourced building sponsored by an enlightened and well travelled patron importing skilled labour from afar could be contemporaneous with one that used local or unskilled labour within a strict budget. Although the lower courses of Restenneth are likely to be significantly older than Markinch, later work may not be. It underlines the need to understand the historical context of a building as well as its architecture and archaeology.

St Vigean's

It is difficult to make any meaningful comparisons between this much altered tower with its long irregularly cut red sandstone blocks and the disciplined coursing of Markinch. However, it is worth noting St Vigean's position in the landscape, sitting on a prominent mound close to running water. It is an important site with a large collection of Pictish stones surviving. Did the Protestant reformers in Markinch, who must have done so much damage to ornamentation on the church, deliberately hide sculptured stones or are they entirely absent from the area (with the possible exception of the mutilated Stob Cross)?

St Margaret's Chapel Edinburgh Castle

This little chapel is a puzzle that has vexed many an observer. Focussing simply upon the decorated arch and ignoring the rest of the building which may be earlier, we immediately pick out a diamond motif familiar from Markinch. It is carved upon the face of a quirked (beaded and grooved) hood moulding similar to the one with a saltire motif found at Markinch in 2014. Unfortunately, it does not help with dating as whilst many aspects of the building point to the early part of the 12th century or even earlier, the arch with its chevron design is likely to postdate similar designs at Durham from slightly later.

Legerwood

Legerwood does not have a tower to compare with Markinch and the following observations relate to the much altered nave and chancel area. The external plinth design is the same on both buildings. The decoration at Legerwood of the internal string courses and capitals is undisciplined and erratic but as we have little to set it alongside at Markinch comparison would be unfair. The overall range of designs at Legerwood, with a beaded double row saltire motif, is very similar to the range at Markinch and we might suspect the masons with similar skills working on both buildings but under different supervision, or perhaps with a less demanding patron.

Both buildings have a good range of masons' marks but with little overlap between them except for the star and simpler forms of cross, arrow and asterisk. There appears to be a capital letter A and a V, both appearing only once. The "bow and arrow" motif is found scattered across England but has not so far been found elsewhere in Scotland. The Corpus of Medieval Scottish Parish Churches ascribes Legerwood to the second quarter of the 12th century on the stylistic evidence of the chancel arch.

St Rule's in St Andrews

The great diversity of buildings in Northern England during the late 11th century and of Scotland during the first half of the 12th century has been remarked upon[2]. This is ascribed to an absence of a strong indigenous building tradition combined with a variety of patrons all drawing upon different architectural resources outside their region. When comparing Markinch and its close neighbour St Rule's we might ask whether one was a development of the other or, conversely, whether their superficial similarity belies the fact that they have very different origins. This section does not attempt to enter into the complex debate around when St Rule's was built although it may provide some additional observations from its near neighbour that might contribute to the debate.

The first and most obvious point of comparison between the two buildings is the height and shape of the tower. St Rule's tower is about one third higher than Markinch and broader by a similar amount. However, whilst Markinch is well proportioned with string courses separating the stages, St Rule's is designed to create the effect of height rather than proportion. This visual impact is reinforced by the lack of string courses between the base and the belfry windows and by the selection of massive blocks around the base from the plinth up to eye level around the tower. Even the blocks higher up the tower are significantly larger than those

[2] Cambridge, E. *Early Romanesque Architecture in North East England* in Rolland et al (1994). & Fearnie, E. Early Church Architecture in Scotland . PSAS 116 (1986)

at Markinch. St Rule's is a showpiece construction as befits a national shrine. Due to extensive erosion or possibly deliberate destruction of ornamentation during the Reformation it is not clear whether or not the single string course at St Rule's was decorated in a fashion similar to the string courses at Markinch.

An interesting contrast between the two buildings is the way the towers join with the rest of the building. At Markinch the nave clasps the tower

firmly with a good overlap and the use of thackstones built into the tower that were designed to protect part of the nave. There is much less overlap and less integration between the two equivalent parts of the St Rule's building, at least at eaves level.

The plinths of the two buildings are very similar but it is believed that the foundations of St Rule's are much deeper than those at Markinch[3]. Given the subsidence observed at Markinch this might indicate either that Markinch was built before St Rule's (and the builders were learning from experience) or that the towers were built by two entirely different teams using different methods of construction.

The structure of the tower is quite different between the two buildings. St Rule's is flanked with two supporting buttresses like many towers in Yorkshire whereas at Markinch the structure relies upon the strength of a thick reinforced lower wall section. The buttresses at St Rule's are specifically designed to support the tower and are not the residual traces of a now lost

3 Fernie, E. PSAS No. 116. (1986). p407

western chamber (although one did once exist as evinced by the inserted western tower arch). The spiral stair, a fundamental feature of Markinch tower, is missing from St Rule's and there may have been a wooden structure at one time, before the existing stairs were installed. It was probably on the south side where two windows are located. Perhaps it was thought that there was little chance of a national shrine being attacked and burned or perhaps it was a matter of economy in such a tall structure.

The similarities between the belfry openings at St Rule's and Markinch have been observed by several writers. They are both unusual in that there is no external framing arch, a pattern found in most other 12th century Scottish towers and the norm throughout the British Isles and beyond. This includes Wharram-le-Street with which St. Rules has been compared[4]. Here, there are

two pillars left of a framing arch that has had its top removed by a rebuilding of the tower's upper stage. The key difference with Markinch is that the central pillar at St Rule's is supported by a lintel at right angles to the wall and passing through its entire thickness. Again, this is an architectural device that has a long pedigree and may have contributed to the belief that the tower was built in the 11th century (compare the belfry window of 11th century St Margaret's Church at Marton in Lincolnshire). At Markinch the internal courses are supported by an internal arch, the outside and the inside facing courses being supported independently.

The windows differ in other respects. On either side of the belfry window Markinch has engaged shafts cut from the same stone block as the surrounding wall. At St Rule's the shafts are now missing but must have been carved independently. Their absence from all windows suggests that they

[4] correspondence between John Bilson and David Hay Fleming St Andrews University Library Special Collections, msdep113/2

may have originally been turned and painted wood that decayed and fell out (the same may even be true of the tower arch on a larger scale). The twin single-stone window arches at St Rule's have two decorative grooves whereas those at Markinch have only one. Finally, the small capitals on top of the pillars at St Rule's are cone shaped with a slight bead, possibly to match the great tower arch, whilst those at Markinch are cushion shaped with sloping cuts or "lunettes" on all three visible sides and no surviving bead. The windows of St Rule's have slat marks where boards would once have been inserted to project the sound of bells in a downward direction. Markinch has no such marks, opening up the possibility that the most brightly lit room in the tower was used for purposes other than housing a bell. The four elegant interior arches within Markinch's belfry stage do not find a parallel at St Rules and seem to have been designed to be seen from inside rather than conventional belfry window arches that are designed to be seen from outside.

All the arches preserved at Markinch, both monolithic and segmented, are of the standard semi-circular Romanesque variety. The architect at St Rule's, however, experiments with a form of parabolic arch above the small door overlooking the nave and with a type of simple "three-centred" arch on the external opening of the nave windows. The nave windows splay both outwards and inwards perhaps deliberately recalling an old Anglo-Saxon style. This is a feature apparently underplayed in the correspondence between John Bilson and David Hay Fleming when the theory of St Rule's links with Wharram was developing in the 1920s.[5] The possibility that the masons at St Rules derived their window design from Markinch rather than Wharram was not considered and cannot be ruled out until both buildings are more firmly dated.

At Markinch we have no nave windows preserved. The windows on the tower are better suited to defence than to external display. The smaller tower windows at St Rule's are straight through tunnel like features whereas at Markinch, with the exception of the small openings above the belfry, they are splayed to the inside in standard "Anglo-Norman" style. Horizontal interior ledges seem to have been cut later, perhaps to accommodate candles or cressets.

5 5 St Andrews University Library Special Collections, msdep113/2

The great tower arches of the two buildings are difficult to compare as we only have full access to the tower side at Markinch and the side of the eastern chamber at St Rule's. The nave side of the tower arch at Markinch is still hidden behind 19th century lath and plaster. Both, however, have a double row of voussoirs although at St Rule's the upper row facing the eastern chamber is stepped forward whereas at Markinch the side of the arch facing the nave is much simpler, at least where we have access towards the crown of the arch. At Markinch this simplicity extends to the overall shape of the arch. It is again, standard Norman Romanesque with no attempt at horseshoe-shaped upper arch or outwardly sloping walls as at St Rule's.

As regards the other two arches at St Rule's, the western and the eastern, there is debate over whether they are original to the building and they have been left out of this comparison. It is worth noting that the remains of the chancel arch at Markinch points to a broad arch designed to frame the ceremonial of the chancel whereas the height and scale of the arches at St Rule's point to a more processional function. This again emphasises the very different functions of the two buildings.

St Drostan's and St. Rule's have therefore both similarities and differences and should perhaps be dated independently of each other. Neither seems to be a simple development of the other in terms of design or execution although there may be a link between belfry openings which without their external framing arch are unusual. With royal patronage, the builder of St Rule's may have drawn upon skilled workmen from within Scotland perhaps with an Anglo-Saxon heritage, although the master mason seems to have been in touch with some sophisticated ideas from outside the British Isles, perhaps Spain.

The patron of Markinch church, however, may well have sent south for skilled labour and employed the best that could be found on the open market. His master mason may even have had experience with military buildings but equally he could have been recruited from a major ecclesiastical site such as Durham, Dunfermline or even some of the early English cathedrals. It is significant that Markinch tower is covered in stonemasons' marks indicating the employment of travelling workers on piecework rates. No masons' marks were found at St Rule's with the possible exception of one on the exterior of the north wall which could in fact be a dedication cross. The masons in St

Andrews may have worked directly for the Bishop or even the Crown on a set price contract, a daily fee or in gangs that were paid on a staged basis.

We leave this comparison with a question. Is Markinch in some way a copy of St Rules or could St Rules have been an attempt by a rival patron to put Markinch in the shade? The rivalry between bishops of St Andrews and earls of Fife is returned to in the chapter dealing with who built Markinch church.

Dunning

Dunning Church may well be Strathearn's equivalent to Markinch, a major place of worship at the heart of the earldom that was donated to an Augustinan Priory in a series of steps during the late 12th and early 13th

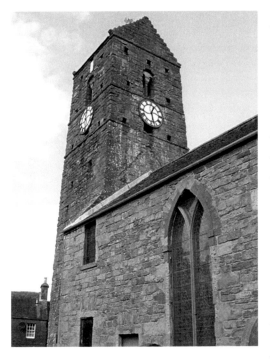

centuries. The parallels continue after the Reformation with both churches rebuilding their frontage to accommodate the new form of religion. In Dunning's case the expansion to the south was later than at Markinch and there was no equivalent expansion to the north thus preserving some features of the 12th century nave and chancel. The original layout of both churches appears to have been very similar but Dunning's nave at 8.3 m is wider than that at Markinch.[6] At 4.65 m the tower is slightly narrower.

Architecturally, the tower at Dunning lacks the modular balance of Markinch, having what appears to be a compressed middle storey between two undecorated string courses. The stonework does not have the disciplined regularity found at Markinch and may have been intended as a base for lime-wash. The tower arch from its design seems to have been inserted in the 13th century and so it is not

---

[6] Corpus of Scottish Medieval Churches, St Andrews University

possible to compare it with the existing original arch at Markinch. The belfry windows at Dunning, as at Dunblane, present voussoir arches to the exterior of the building unlike Markinch where they face inwards. The small single-stone arches are supported by through-stones as at St Rules and Dunblane but in contrast to Markinch. They may represent the use of more traditional building techniques rather than an earlier build but much more comparative work needs to be carried out following Semple's pioneering work.

The earls of Strathearn, particularly Ferteth and Gille-Brigte, were close to the summit of Scottish nobility and the history of the Dunning Church (as well as nearby Muthill) is likely to be linked to the family fortunes. Except perhaps during their minority, only the earls of Fife were higher in terms of rank and this may be reflected in the quality of the three buildings.

Muthill

At Muthill we appear to have something very different from Markinch - a medieval church built around an earlier free standing tower. In contrast to Markinch the tower has been altered many times and seems to have a later Romanesque upper storey added, complete with three pillared belfry openings (on two sides at least).[7] The tower's architecture has been carefully assessed by Semple but not compared directly to Markinch. Renovations include the insertion of a west door at ground level and substantial renovations to the walls. The present author would suggest the possibility that the diamond motif has been applied later to an earlier plain string course as individual elements of the design are spread across adjacent stones. Although this cannot be proved it cautions us against dating the

entire tower on the basis of a single decorative feature. Despite the fact that they are regularly grouped together[8], one of the few things that Markinch and Muthill towers have in common is the simple fact that they are towers. Markinch tower may have been designed with secondary defensive capabilities but Muthill tower looks as if its  original primary purpose was one of defence or perhaps the protection of secular treasure. It seems to have had an internal wooden staircase[9].

As with Dunning, Muthill's tower is slightly narrower than that at Markinch - 4.67m (15' 3") and it is smaller at 15.64m (51' 4"). It has no great arch facing into the nave, only a small door that looks as if it had been modified. Another small west facing door with a simple segmental arch has been blocked and may also have been an addition. Its three tiers are slightly set back but not clearly defined with projecting string courses. The stonework in many parts is competent but overall the work lacks the consistency and discipline that is found at Markinch. Semple dates the tower to between 1108 and 1122.

Dunfermline Abbey Church

As with St Rule's we are comparing Markinch to a much larger building with a very different function, although at least in Dunfermline's case we know that building was begun around 1128, overlapping with the later stages of nave construction at Durham. Dunfermline was probably nearing completion when it was dedicated in 1150.

The sample of stonemasons' marks located at Dunfermline is not large (7-8) and the majority are relatively simple in form but most are also to be

8 eg MacQuarrie, 2013 A. Medieval Scotland : Kingship and Nation

9 Semple, M-C. (2012)

found at Markinch. As regards stone carving no examples of lozenge decoration were found at Dunfermline but good examples of complex chip-carved saltire motif with a quirked edge are found on both buildings used in different contexts. At Markinch the motif is used in the chancel hood moulding found in 2014, whereas at Dunfermline the

Dunfermline (West Door)

design is found in several of the capitals of the west door. It might be noted that the mason at Dunfermline used a similar pattern of intersecting saltires to the one used on the arch at Markinch although there are subtle differences. It is also possible that some of the stones in the west door at Dunfermline are recycled from the earlier church.

St Magnus Cathedral

Donaldson[10] notes that by 1137 when the cathedral at Kirkwall was started there were already many Norman style churches in Scotland. St Magnus is a complex building evolving over many decades. It was examined in detail during the course of the survey but little of relevance to Markinch was discovered. It does, however, demonstrate that by the 1130s a highly sophisticated piece of Romanesque construction could arise at a great distance from the main centres of building activity in Normandy and southern England.

Dunblane

This is another originally freestanding tower that seems to have been extended upwards and integrated into a later ecclesiastical building. It clearly belongs to a different building tradition to Muthill despite the similarities between the belfry windows on the two towers. Compared to Markinch there

---

[10] Donaldson G. 1988 *The Contemporary Scene* Introductory chapter in Crawford, B. (ed) 1988

has been a less disciplined approach to the cutting and half-bonding of the stones. The irregularity of shape and colour may indicate a different stone-working tradition, different geological conditions in the quarry or simply a lower budget. Again, as at Muthill and Dunning, the voussoired arch is presented to the outside in contrast to Markinch. The cushion capitals at Dunblane, if original, have a heavy bead or astragal around the top of the column in contrast to Markinch where, unusually, the bead is absent or eroded.

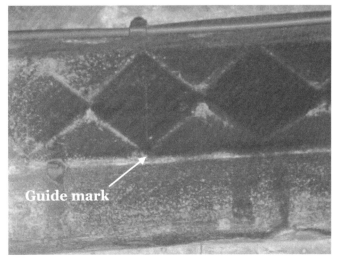

Close inspection of the hood moulding above a recessed arch inside the tower (above right) reveals that the pattern of the lozenge decoration has been laid out using the same technique of vertical scoring (guide mark) as is found on the internal string course at Leuchars (see below right) dated to the central decades of the 12th century[11] and at Kirkburn in Yorkshire dated to the second quarter of the 12th century. Markinch may have had something similar on its string courses but it is now too eroded to compare effectively. The lozenge banding at Muthill, despite the close links with Dunblane, is cut in a completely different

[11] Corpus of Scottish Medieval Parish Churches

way and, as noted above, may be a secondary application. No masons' marks were found at Dunblane but the diagonal tooling is of a high standard. The internal chamfered support arch at Dunblane is also similar to that found at the base of the tower at Kirkburn and Grimston in Yorkshire.

Given that it features on a number of 12th century Scottish buildings, the lozenge motif is worth considering more closely[12]. It may have had some kind of symbolic significance perhaps among the native clergy, as the design pattern does not seem to be prominent in buildings associated with imported monastic orders[13]. However, it is also occasionally used as a decorative motif in England[14] including externally on the south transept at Durham.

Leuchars

Again we have a chancel and apse surviving that cannot be compared with Markinch where they are absent. Neither is there any evidence for an apse at Markinch. The lozenge motif appears again at Leuchars and the technique of its application with vertical guidelines scratched across the surface of the lozenges is similar to Dunblane. There is little overlap of masons' marks between the two buildings although the V mark, one of the candidates for the senior mason at Markinch, recurs at Leuchars. The exuberance of the designs on the arches at Leuchars suggests that the patron is trying to compete in terms of display. Unfortunately, given the loss of the chancel arch at Markinch, we cannot compare the two directly, although the patron could well have been a close MacDuff kinsman[15].

[12] This includes Dunblane, Leuchars, Muthill, Tynninghame and St Margaret's Chapel. Brechin Tower has a single diamond below the door opposite the crucified Christ.

[13] King, M. The Kilbroney Cross, the Book of Kells and an Early Christian Symbol of the Resurrection

[14] e.g. St Giles, Risby Suffolk, & St Edmund, Stoulton, Worcs.

[15] Possibly Ness son of Willam alive between 1150 and 1175

Dalmeny

Much of what applies to Leuchars also applies to Dalmeny, although the interior decoration is not quite as highly decorated. The differences between the collections of masons' marks at Dalmeny and Markinch is greater than that between Leuchars and Markinch. Dalmeny displays a higher proportion of fully formed letters most of which have serifs or added strokes. Two, as at Dunfermline are double lined but these must have been recycled from an ancillary building, possibly the tower which is now absent. These are discussed later but the implication is that Dalmeny was built either by a group stonemasons demonstrating a degree of

literacy or Dalmeny is chronologically later than Markinch, built at a time when masons were beginning to take pride in personalising their work to a greater degree.

Birnie in Moray

Despite its small size, Birnie church is well built and for a while had cathedral status within the locality and was a Bishop's seat before Elgin. The lobed and scalloped chancel capitals are similar in some respects to those at Legerwood. At Dunning we see a reused fragment in the front wall that may be part of a similar capital but with concave lobes. The capital at Markinch is missing and the reconstruction drawing leaves this part of the arch blank until a capital is unearthed, although the

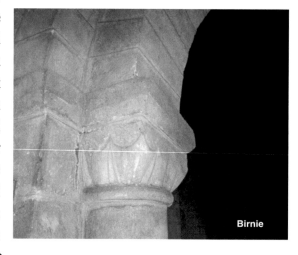
Birnie

possibility of the chancel arch capitals having an engaged volute form cannot be ruled out in light of the survival of a carved piece reused under the Session House canopy. The plinths at Markinch and Birnie are close matches. It is not known whether Birnie had a tower.

Tyninghame

The remains here are relatively sophisticated and imaginative but features such as the scalloped apse arch capital and the chip-cut lozenge decoration

tie in with other perhaps earlier Scottish churches already discussed. In fact the impost with its rows of lozenges above one of the capitals repeats two of the Markinch motifs. Like Dalmeny and Leuchars, Tyninghame features chevron decorations on the arches reflecting a style most probably made popular after Durham and perhaps Dunfermline Abbey Church had been completed. No trace of such decoration has been found at Markinch but the remains are scarce.

Garvald and Bara

All that remains of this small church in East Lothian that is relevant to Markinch is the lozenge design on the string course and the decorative effect cut into a single stone arch reset into the interior. The church is historically linked with the nuns of North Berwick. It is worth noting the reused fragment of window arch inside the building with its incised decoration, again reminiscent of Markinch belfry windows.

Bonkle, Berwickshire

Little remains at Bonkle but a very simple 12th century arch with undecorated imposts attached to an earlier apse.

The masons' marks are of interest, however, and those few that are represented are not unlike those on the lower stages of Markinch tower.

St Magnus Church Egilsay

This has a round tower but the overall layout of nave and chancel appears similar to St Drostan's Markinch. Of particular note is the small doorway giving access from the tower to the nave roof space. Eric Fernie interprets this as a door that led onto a wooden gallery across the west end of the nave designed for an ecclesiastical or lay magnate.[16] He also refers to an upper chapel above the chancel, a part of the building which of course is missing at Markinch. He also observes that the building was constructed around a modular unit of just under 15 feet (4.54m) whilst at Markinch the unit appears to be 16 and a half feet (5.03m).

11th and 12th Century Churches in the North of England

Weaverthorpe, Yorkshire

Like Markinch, Weaverthorpe has a high unadorned tower arch, a chamfered base and perhaps significantly, a tower of exactly the same width (16 ft 6 ins). However, the stones are smaller, the arch has only a single row of voussoirs and the belfry openings are more akin to Dunblane and Dunning than to Markinch and St Rule's. It has no west door but does have a high centrally positioned doorway looking down into the nave (or giving access to a former loft or clerestory).

[16] Fernie, E. 1988 *St Magnus Church Egilsay* in *St Magnus Cathedral*, Crawford, B. (Ed.)

Wharram-le-Street

This is a tiny Yorkshire church that has been compared to the great national monument at St Rule's. This is based upon the general form of the belfry windows and the unusual arch shape as well as documented links between Bishop Robert of Scone (who is recorded as being involved in rebuilding work at St Rule's) and the now vanished Augustinian Nostell Priory to which Wharram was given in the 1120s. It is a debate that need not concern us here. As far as Markinch is concerned the double saltire pattern, seen on the recently found chancel hood-moulding segment, is replicated on a chancel arch impost at Wharram, probably on a part that was updated to suit Anglo-Norman tastes. The tower is slightly narrower than

Markinch's at 15 ft 6 ins, akin to Muthil.

Kirkburn, Yorkshire

Kirkburn has some lozenge chip-carving reminiscent of the string course at Markinch but with much chevron decoration and billet hood moulding on the chancel arch the church is closer to Leuchars in style.

Durham Cathedral

It may seem inappropriate to compare a parish church, even one described once as "a minster" with a cathedral but, unlike most smaller churches, the work at Durham is relatively well documented from the laying of the foundation stone in 1093 until the completion of the high vault in 1133. The regular laying of the stones in half-bonded fashion is perhaps the most striking similarity with Markinch although other features such as the rubble vaulting above the spiral stairs[17] and the use of external decorated external string courses are worth noting. Particularly interesting in terms of Markinch is the use of decorated string courses although these were not an innovation at Durham.

Most of the masons" marks found at Markinch are also to be of be found at Durham whereas relatively few of the marks found at Dalmeny are also found at Durham. However, in the absence of specific "fingerprinting" of the work of individual masons this need not be as significant as it first appears. Also, the marks collected at Durham were not collected under the rigorous conditions imposed at Markinch. We must therefore set this aside as an interesting area for further research.

Although the scale of Markinch and Durham are very different the quality and alignment of the sandstone masonry is very similar. The link may, however, be via the church at Dunfermline. More research is required, particularly into the methods of measurement in the two buildings. Mortar samples and wall thicknesses could also be compared.

Examples from the South of England

It would be possible to take this or that detail from Markinch and find close parallels with similar details from the many hundreds of 12th century churches scattered across the south of England, but these could be random occurrences. A couple of examples are chosen here to demonstrate particular points relating to design.

It has been mentioned that the diamond motif is relatively rare in England compared to Scotland but Risby in Suffolk not only has a good example but

---

[17] McAleer, J. P. *The West Front of Durham Cathedral (p. 207)* in Rollandson et al 1994

displays it internally in two bands along an impost or string course similar to that surrounding Markinch tower. The commentator ascribes a relatively early date to the string course : *The tower arch, to judge from its proportions and the arch profile, must date from c.1090-1110, and there is no reason to suppose that the capitals and imposts are not original.* [18]

Another example, St Leonard's Southoe, this time from Huntingdonshire where David I had landholding interests, combines the curved saltire motif with the diamond motif. Baxter dates this doorway to around 1100 demonstrating how early these simple designs were developed.

As already noted the motif of the intersecting saltires is commonly found throughout Europe, the earliest example found during this survey being an 11th century voussoir from Caen in Normandy (eg the northern transept arch of La Trinité).   The survey examined over 140 examples using the online database the *Corpus of Romanesque Sculpture of Britain and Ireland* and no single example incorporated all the features of the section of hood moulding found at Markinch. The nearest was a section of string course at St Peter's Peterchurch Herefordshire. Here, the main arches incorporate both chevron design and the saltire motif with a double bead although the chamfer is hollow. The tower arch, doorway and string course are "described as *"likely to be between c.1120 and c.1140, when chip-carving was becoming old-fashioned and chevron gaining in popularity.[19]"*

Those interested in visual comparisons are invited to visit the *Corpus* website where excellent images are available. It should be noted, however, that the website does not deal with defensive structures and there are many useful comparisons that can be gleaned from the 12th century remains of secular buildings such as Norham Castle in Northumberland attributed to c 1121.[20]

Irish Comparisons

So far, individual details have been compared but in the case of Cormac's Chapel in Cashel it is the overall appearance of the tower that is striking.[21] It

---

[18] Dr Ron Baxter *Corpus of Romanesque Sculpture in Britain and Ireland*

[19] Dr Ron Baxter *op cit*

[20] Pearson. T. and Ainsworth S. English Heritage Survey Report of Norham Castle 2002

[21] Photograph with kind permission of Department of Arts, Heritage, Gaeltacht and the Islands'

seems to have been heightened at some stage but the lower half with its decorated string course resembles Markinch tower without the belfry windows. Furthermore, the string courses continue around the nave and chancel at eaves height as is believed to be the case at Markinch. Begun in 1124 and consecrated in 1134, it shows that a relatively sophisticated building could, given the right conditions, spring up on the fringes of Europe. Furthermore, the building was the result of a king of Munster whose rank in Ireland was in some ways akin to the MacDuff Clan Chief in Scotland. To further complicate the picture, despite the that much of the chapel is still standing, architectural historians disagree over the architectural influences on the building - Salisbury, Western France, Regensburg, or even Ewenny in Wales.[22]. As far as Markinch is concerned, the decorated string course, perhaps even a direct echo from late 11th century Normandy, is worth remarking upon. Internally, the lozenge decoration is the dominant motif. Sculpted volute capitals are interspersed with simpler versions of cushion capital (photo copyright Department of Arts, Heritage, Gaeltacht and the Islands).

Continental Comparisons

We have few scraps of information left in terms of architectural detail at Markinch but the belfry windows are an exception. Despite the inevitable erosion, they appear to be more or less intact and still show signs of a simple line decoration on their single stone arches. Paired belfry windows without a framing arch and without a through-wall lintel supporting the twin monolithic arches are unusual within the British Isles. St. Rule's comes close

---

[22] O'Keeffe, T. (2003) *Romanesque Ireland: architecture and ideology in the twelfth century,* Academia

in terms of comparison but does have a through lintel. Some churches in Sussex[23] have no framing arch and no through lintel but lack the flanking pillars. The closest continental match found in terms of the different architectural elements in fact comes from Normandy in France. The *chevet* or apse-like appendage of the late 11th century church (1083) of St Nicholas-des-Champs near Caen in Normandy (below left) has an external arcade very close in appearance and structure to the paired window lights at Markinch.

Here the difference is in terms of the design of the capitals, simple foliate instead of cushion. It is worth remarking upon the use of the "eyebrow" decoration[24] on the single-stone arches and the way that the engaged flanking columns appear to be set flush with the wall surface.

We must of course be cautious with such comparisons. Similarities may be the result of co-incidence or the designs could have made its way into a pattern book used by a master mason. Equally, the window could have been a copy from a now lost example elsewhere in the British Isles such as Holy Trinity Priory, Aldgate[25] or Scone Priory. Eleventh and twelfth century Europe was a place where elites within states were closely interlinked, where ideas travelled fast and we cannot rule out a direct connection with Normandy or a derivative building in England for the master mason at Markinch. A direct Normandy link would of course allow the possible construction period to be pushed back further than Dunfermline or Durham, perhaps to the first quarter of the 12th century, but such a chronology would require further supporting evidence from a period of Scottish history where evidence is lacking.

[23] St Andrews Bishopstone (east window) and St Laurence, Guestling

[24] Also found at St Margaret's Marton in Lincolnshire which has arched eyebrow decoration

[25] founded by Matilda of Scotland in the early 12th century

Conclusion

A number of churches from different parts of the British Isles were inspected, some of which are referred to above but the following notes are observations rather than the analysis of a trained architectural historian. In Scotland, it is difficult to place existing buildings in a chronological sequence. There are a number of reasons for this. Each building, whilst following a general set of principles, was a unique combination of the patron's requirements and resources, the master mason's background and abilities combined with the skills and often the imagination of the work teams. There were many chance factors including the patron's wider social contacts and even which skilled workmen happened to be passing by a particular area at a particular time. There does appear to have been a tradition of freestone building in Scotland, including one employing cut stone and mortar but when the elite sought the highest quality finish to their buildings they seem to have looked outside the country for the requisite skills.

The oldest towers may well have had a secular function providing safety for the *mormaer's* most valued possessions. Some appear to have been adapted in the 12th century to serve an ecclesiastical function (e.g. Muthill, Dunblane). Other high status towers such as Dunning and Markinch seem to have been built with a primarily ecclesiastical function but with an eye to their defensive or protective capabilities. In addition, the families with the deepest pockets or the closest contacts within the royal court could presumably reach further afield for skilled craftsmen. All this makes their various architectural elements extremely difficult to unravel, particularly when the same quarries and in some cases the same masons were being used. Without good archaeology, sequential dating based upon architectural detail will always provide only part of the story.

Looking beyond Scotland, it is worth noting certain similarities in terms of Markinch's remaining features. Whilst the chip-carved saltire design is found throughout Western Europe from the 11th century, it appears to have declined during the 12th century. Its use with a quirked edge, as at Markinch, may compare with some early 12th century decoration in England. It ties in with its use at Dunfermline in the early 1130s unless the carved the stones in question were recycled from the earlier building. As regards the string course decoration, given its importance to the design of Markinch and the frequency of its occurrence in Scotland, the lozenge motif is worth investigating further.

However, it is not particularly useful in pinning down the date of the building as examples exist of decorated string courses in high status buildings throughout the 12th century. Hidden constructional features are also worth noting such as the width of the tower being 16 feet 6 inches and the width of the nave being half as wide again and this may in the long term be as important as design features in tracing the pedigree of the building. "Fingerprinted" masons' marks may one day also provide part of the picture.

Against this background, although we may be able to point to similarities and differences between individual 12th century buildings throughout the Britain, we should not expect to be able to line them up chronologically from most primitive to most sophisticated as we might today with the motor car or the space rocket. There were certainly technological and design breakthroughs during this period but their impact upon individual buildings was erratically distributed across the country. The castle building programme that swept across much of England in the train of Norman advance must surely have brought about better lifting engines and more standardisation. However, the basic tools of the stonemason remained the same, and when applied to church buildings, technology was a lesser factor when set against the skills and knowledge of a particular workforce combined with the resources and ambition of the person who commissioned the building. A particular patron may even have insisted upon incorporating features in his building that were reminiscent of an earlier age or, alternatively, exotic features that he had observed on pilgrimage to Rome or even in illuminated manuscripts. What counted most were the resources, both human and financial, that he could draw upon.

All of the architectural features found at Markinch could have been a feature of a high status building somewhere in Europe from the earliest years of the 12th century, and most were still being incorporated into lesser buildings in the latter years of the century. Against this background we have to satisfy ourselves with "best fit" and partial explanations unless compelling historical or archaeological evidence proves otherwise. A decade and a half ago expert opinion placed Markinch church in the second quarter of the 12th century. More recent estimates place it more towards the middle[26] and end[27]. The pendulum could easily swing back to the beginning of the century as we

---

[26] Fawcett, Professor R. 2002, 2011

[27] Places of Worship in Scotland. Scottish Church Heritage Research Ltd (website 3/7/16)

come to understand more fully the intermeshing of Scottish, English and Anglo-Norman elites during the period following the death of Malcolm III. There is no intrinsic reason why an early Scottish building connected to an elite family should not draw upon the skills and design traditions of 11th century Normandy in the same way as those much further south. On the other hand the discovery on site of an elaborately carved voussoir with chevron design could push the possible date further towards the end of the century.

We can conclude that Markinch tower does not fit in neatly with any progression of building types from within Scotland, but draws its inspiration from outside. More specifically this inspiration is from the Anglo-Norman world and from a period prior to the elaborate stone-carving show pieces of Leuchars and Dalmeny which in turn drew their inspiration from the later work at Durham and Dunfermline. There would appear to be nothing in Markinch's repertoire of design features that rules out an early date if we assume that the builder had the resources to cast his net widely for skilled workmen and master masons. All we can say at present in terms of architectural history is that the remains of the building at Markinch represent either very high quality example from the early part of the 12th century or a competent building from later in that century.

Our inability to pinpoint a date for Markinch based upon design features should come as no surprise. There are many buildings in a state much more complete than Markinch which are a puzzle in terms of dating and, with the exception of cathedrals, a firm dating from this period is rare. What is encouraging with respect to Markinch is that the historical fog surrounding the period within which it was built is beginning to clear, thanks to some recent scholarship into the Fife elites and their close links to the Crown. Much more effort is required, adding to our increased historical knowledge with scientific analysis such as carbon 14 and dendrochronology dating as a backup to good archeology.

Scotland and the North of England have an excellent 12th century architectural heritage despite almost a thousand years of destruction. Whilst important work is continuing on Scotland's broader medieval church heritage,[28] there is a need for a simple, portable and well-illustrated guide to

[28] A Corpus of Scottish Medieval Parish Churches, School of Art History, University of St Andrews
Places of Worship in Scotland, Scottish Church Heritage Research

some of the scattered examples of Romanesque sculpture and architecture throughout Scotland. It is now over thirty years since a husband and wife team produced *Ecosse Romane*[29] in French, and a modern replacement in English aimed at the general public is overdue, perhaps covering Northumberland and Durham as well.

[29] Sharrat, France and Peter (1985)

Chapter 6

6. Comparison of Stonemasons' Marks
The enigmatic legacy of the workers

During June and July 2015 a team led by Moira Greig analysed in some detail over 800 marks located throughout the 12th century church tower at Markinch[1]. As well as providing a comprehensive collection of marks for Markinch, she has demonstrated convincingly that many of the marks have been used at different times in history proving that a single mark *per se* cannot be ascribed to a particular individual.

This chapter attempts to take the survey a step further by comparing the results with other 12th century buildings in the East of Scotland, assembling the data collected from Leuchars, Dalmeny and Legerwood (where a plaster wall coating prevented a full survey being carried out). The churches all appear from the best evidence available to date from the the 12th century but

---

[1] Greig, Moira. St Drostan's Church, Markinch, Fife. A Survey of Masons' Marks within the Tower. For Markinch Heritage Group July 2015

no secure dating is available at this time. Detailed drawings of each mark found are reproduced in Appendices 1 and 2.

Other late 11th and early 12th century churches have been examined where no or very few marks were found (St Serf's on Loch Leven, St Margarets Edinburgh, St Vigeans, Restenneth, Tynninghame, Muthill, Dunning and St Rule's). No systematic work has so far been undertaken at Dunblane but the lower part of the tower is without marks. It is assumed that different payment systems for work undertaken prevailed at these sites or that stone marking was either obliterated or cut on hidden facets of the blocks. Marks do exist at Dunfermline Abbey Church but insufficient data was collected to draw reasonable conclusions.

It is assumed throughout this section that the prime function of the marks was to attribute individual pieces of work to particular masons or teams of masons for purposes of payment. Other marks and graffiti were observed but are not included.

Method

With one hundred percent samples of visible marks available from the Markinch tower survey and from a survey[2] of Dalmeny (nave, chancel and arch), it was decided to take a comparable sixty percent sample from Leuchars (mainly chancel and apse). The Leuchars sample omits marks above the internal string course of the chancel which are too high to photograph but includes a few recently uncovered marks from recycled material that would once have been in situ within the nave. This enables all three buildings to be compared although the limitations of the sampling process must be accepted. A survey of Legerwood's remaining chancel was carried out but the building was clearly smaller than the other three, exhibiting only five sets of distinctive marks plus two letters used only once. It has therefore been omitted from the diagram showing the overlapping of marks but included in the tables. This method enables projects to be compared as a whole across the full spectrum of marks and is designed to avoid the natural tendency to look for similarities rather than differences.

---

[2] A. J. Turner, (1948) Study kept in Dalmeny nave

1. Masons' marks found at Markinch and Dalmeny
(number and percentage of marks)

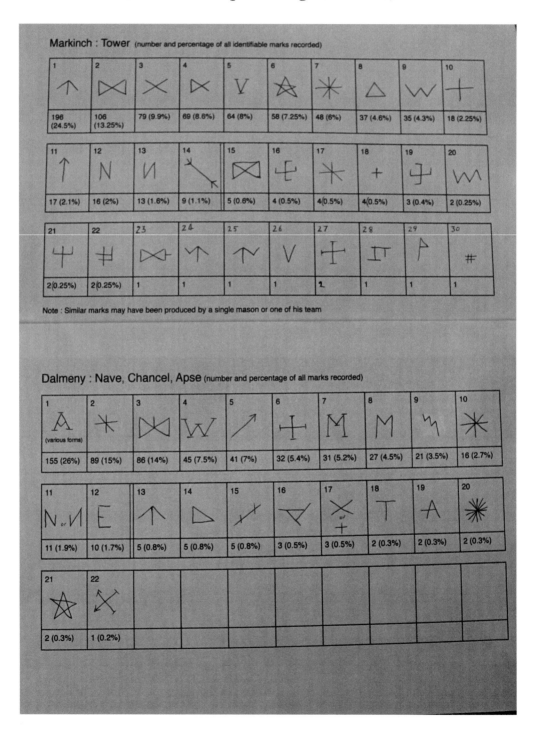

2. Masons' marks found at Leuchars and Legerwood
(number and percentage of marks)

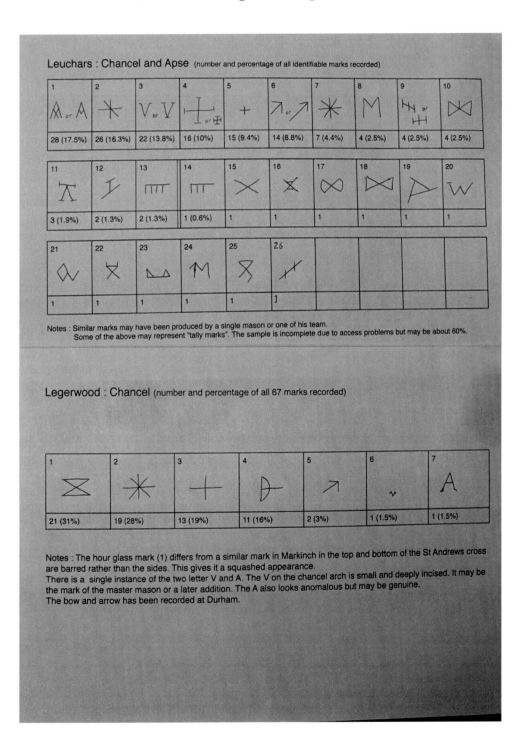

Leuchars : Chancel and Apse (number and percentage of all identifiable marks recorded)

1	2	3	4	5	6	7	8	9	10
28 (17.5%)	26 (16.3%)	22 (13.8%)	16 (10%)	15 (9.4%)	14 (8.8%)	7 (4.4%)	4 (2.5%)	4 (2.5%)	4 (2.5%)

11	12	13	14	15	16	17	18	19	20
3 (1.9%)	2 (1.3%)	2 (1.3%)	1 (0.6%)	1	1	1	1	1	1

21	22	23	24	25	26				
1	1	1	1	1	1				

Notes : Similar marks may have been produced by a single mason or one of his team.
Some of the above may represent "tally marks". The sample is incomplete due to access problems but may be about 60%.

Legerwood : Chancel (number and percentage of all 67 marks recorded)

1	2	3	4	5	6	7
21 (31%)	19 (28%)	13 (19%)	11 (16%)	2 (3%)	1 (1.5%)	1 (1.5%)

Notes : The hour glass mark (1) differs from a similar mark in Markinch in the top and bottom of the St Andrews cross are barred rather than the sides. This gives it a squashed appearance.
There is a single instance of the two letter V and A. The V on the chancel arch is small and deeply incised. It may be the mark of the master mason or a later addition. The A also looks anomalous but may be genuine.
The bow and arrow has been recorded at Durham.

It should be noted that in the diagram all "arrow" marks are grouped together as it was not possible to distinguish two different variations at Leuchars and Dalmeny as had been the case at Markinch. The N or Z marks appear to be significantly different at Markinch and Dalmeny where they have one leg shorter than the other. The A-type marks at Leuchars have no serifs or appendage marks whilst those at Dalmeny, despite their variability do have such marks. There may be two forms of "tepee" mark at Markinch, one based upon the saltire and the other upon the conventional cross.

It should also be noted that the samples are taken from different parts of the buildings (Markinch tower, Leuchars chancel and apse, Dalmeny nave and chancel) although this should not significantly affect the results. The Venn diagram diagram also omits marks that are unclear and rarely occurring marks (>1%).

Results

It is generally believed that all four buildings were constructed during the 12th century[3] and links with both Durham and Dunfermline have been suggested. All of the buildings displayed marks that have been recorded for

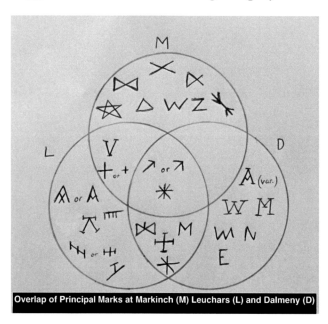

Overlap of Principal Marks at Markinch (M) Leuchars (L) and Dalmeny (D)

Durham[4] but there were many marks recorded that have so far not been noted at Durham indicating the need for further research on this potentially key link. Additionally, the methodology used in collecting the marks at Durham is not clear and is unlikely to approach the rigour of the work at, for example, Markinch.

Each of the three larger

[3] A Corpus of Medieval Scottish Parish Churches. St Andrews University

[4] Waples, William. 1937-47

buildings seems to have had a core of around a dozen regularly used marks. These represent over 90% of the marks recorded in each case. There is only a limited amount of overlap between the core team marks at the three sites. Only the arrow and the asterisk were commonly used at all three sites. Other isolated cross marks may relate to later dedications.

The diagram could be interpreted in several ways. The large number of marks that are unique to each building could indicate :-

(i) that we are dealing with three quite distinct project work groups recruited independently of each other from different pools of labour or,

(ii) that the three work groups were recruited at different time periods.

(iii) the workers were recruited from the same pool of labour at the same time

By contrast the marks common to all three could indicate either :-

(i)   that all of the projects were carried out within the working life of the masons who regularly used these marks and worked on the buildings sequentially.

(ii) That they were relatively common marks perhaps allocated to novice masons at the start of a project.

(iii) that they were marks spread over a wide time period but handed down from father to son or master to apprentice

Whatever system was used, and these may have varied from one part of the country to another, we must remember that we are dealing with complex patterns of human behaviour not rigid mathematical formulae. Without knowing the rules and working practices of the masons on the ground it is like trying to read hieroglyphics without the Rosetta Stone as a key.

Of the many options, the most likely scenario, at least in 12th century Scotland, may have been that a master mason had a list of relatively simple marks that he distributed when a project began allowing him to distinguish between masons' work for purposes of payment. He himself and a few other experienced masons may have their own mark that they brought to the project but there would essentially be a mix of allocated and personal marks at any one time. During the course of the project other "time-served" masons would arrive at the project with their own distinctive mark and use it as an indication of quality as well as identity. In Scotland it may have been well into the 14th century before all marks were unique to an individual but much more comparative work needs to be done.

This would fit the Markinch pattern for which we have sequential data. All the marks at the bottom of the tower are simple two or three stroke symbols with the exception of one, the serifed capital V made up from five strokes. This additional degree of complexity may suggest that he had a higher status than the others. Further up the tower the work group appears to be joined by a "bow tie" or "hour glass" mark made up from four strokes. The mark is arrived at after a series of approximations by the mason but once formed is strictly adhered to and applied in a manner that allows it to be "fingerprinted" or uniquely identified by the way it is cut (see opposing photographs below). The first chisel stroke of his mark seems to run parallel with his cross hatching. Unfortunately this mason is not found to have unequivocally applied his mark to any of the other buildings in the survey. Moira Greig argues from other evidence in the tower that he was the master mason and he certainly appears to have had a high status. On two separate occasions his mark is accompanied on the same stone by a separate mark. However, his mark is not present on the lower stages of the tower. Probably neither V nor "bow-tie" belonged to the overall master mason who would most probably have been preoccupied by supervision, payment, client liaison and forward planning but that is another discussion.

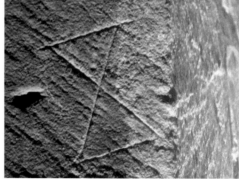

Individual Comparisons by Building

The most notable overlap between Markinch and Leuchars was the serifed letter V (although it may be inverted) and we might speculate that a particular mason who used this mark moved from one site to the other at some time in his career. However, there are slight differences between the application of the mark on the two buildings. The alternative explanation that it was a commonly used mark is less likely because of its complexity although identical complex marks are to be found all across Europe and at widely varying time period. The possible family ties between the patrons of these two buildings might be noted in this context. Ness, son of William, the possible builder of Leuchars, is believed to have been a member of the MacDuff family. However, given the working life of a mason this could simply indicate that Leuchars and Markinch were built anything up to 30 years of each other or by father and son using a similar mark.

There is a clearer overlap of marks between Leuchars and Dalmeny with four clearly shared between them. This might not have been be expected

Dalmeny - Letter marks with serifs

given the distance between the two sites. It may indicate that there was less in the way of a time gap between the projects with several masons or teams of masons moving on within a reasonable span of time from one site to another. Dalmeny, however, compared with both Leuchars and Markinch, displays a high proportion of marks that are letters either with or without serif marks.

There is, by contrast, little overlap at all between the core team marks at Markinch and Dalmeny (other than the simple marks already referred to) indicating a longer time gap between the two construction periods or recruitment from very different pools of labour.

A sizeable number of infrequently used marks at all three sites (>1%) appears to represent temporary workers staying on the site for short periods of time, although we should remember that they could have been transferred briefly from parts of the building that were under construction but that no longer exist. If we are to assume that a skilled mason cut two blocks in a day[5] then these itinerant workers were staying for less than a week and may have been passing through from one project to another, earning their board and lodging as they travelled. Interestingly, these infrequently used marks are fairly unique to each site and do not demonstrate a constant flow between the three sites.

An Examination of the Marks - Evidence of Differentiation

Looking at the form of the marks themselves, we notice that they are based upon very simple forms to which additional lines or serifs may have been added. Generally, the marks at Markinch are simpler than those at Dalmeny, and table 1 shows that there may be a pattern worth exploring further. It seems to show that additional tags were added to basic forms either on the site itself (as with the W at Markinch where a tagged version is found further up the tower) or between one project and another (as with the inverted V's and A's at Leuchars.

The pattern is particularly interesting at Markinch where the simplest of forms (for example the St Andrews cross) are associated with incremental developments of these forms - one stroke for the elongated "tepee" or "picnic table" and two strokes for the "hour glass". In a similar way, the simple cross at Markinch may have been differentiated by converting it into a right angled "tepee" which is later further differentiated at Leuchars with the addition of an extra leg and a pair of "horns".

If this pattern is accepted then the obvious question is did the marks occur organically as individual masons found that they arrived at a site and had to find a mark for themselves that could not be confused with that of a workmate, or was there a master mason who allocated marks perhaps according to a written template? Alternatively do the tags indicate a master-

---

[5] This was discussed with present day stonemasons during the course of the project

apprentice relationship or even family ties? Might the master have taken the opportunity to embellish his mark leaving his old mark to the apprentice? The further study of the many forms of the capital letter "A" at Dalmeny might help us with this. The number of variations seems to suggest a team that was perhaps paid through a single individual but more work is required on this interesting mark.

Before we draw too may conclusions from this suggested set of practices it is worth considering the late arrival of three marks to the Markinch building project that do not appear to fit into any neat pattern. A very broad slash with two inward facing arrows is to be found at Markinch (see chapter 3) but so far no other example applied in this way has been found in Scotland or at Durham. It may be a development of the simple arrow but its style suggests a degree of individualism. A later example has recently been identified at Cambuskenneth but it is applied in a different way. The star motif appears half way up the tower at Markinch and again gives the appearance of a mason arriving, perhaps from a distant site with his own ready made and very distinctive mark. Despite its complexity the star is a common mark across Europe and across time and we should not draw too many conclusions about its use across different sites.

The Use of Marks on a Single Building

All the above analysis shows that we must be careful with our assumptions when comparing one building with another. The marks do, however, reflect a clear sequence of activity when they are applied to a particular building, beginning at the lower courses and working upwards. Some key masons were active at Markinch tower throughout the lifespan of the project whereas other members of the core team came and went, probably on a seasonal basis. When set alongside other evidence such as changes in construction methods this has enabled us to us to estimate how long the tower took to construct.

The evidence so far at Markinch tower points to a very well organised system using standardised blocks assembled in half-bonded fashion that may have been complete in a few seasons (the nave and chancel may have taken longer). This may reflect working practices developed though the rapid construction of defensive structures, particularly in Wales and Northern England rather than ecclesiastical buildings. As noted in a previous chapter, the technique was impressed upon the workers at Markinch by a diagram on a stone showing the entire project team how blocks should be cut and laid to provide maximum strength and speed of construction.

Instruction on half-bonding technique

At Dalmeny Turner believed that the evidence pointed to the various components of the church building (choir, apse and nave) being constructed sequentially rather than concurrently.[6] The same is likely to have been the case at Markinch with perhaps the tower being first to be built, although proof of this will be difficult to find given the loss of nave and chancel.

Unmarked stones

It is worth noting that although most stones at all three main sites would once have had an incised mark there were many that did not. It has been argued that this is the result of marks being chiseled on hidden surfaces but this is unlikely. Any standard stone block would have been cut with at least four surfaces that are now hidden in addition to the visible face. If marks had been randomly applied to all five of these surfaces then we would expect only about one fifth (20%) of the stones to have a visible mark. The exact percentage marked on the face is difficult to calculate because of weathering and spalling but it is well above that figure in all three cases.

Some stones have clear surface dressing marks but no apparent mason's mark. Unmarked stones may be explained by the payment system. Workers may have assembled their stones at the quarry or on site for payment at regular intervals by a paymaster. His late arrival would have held up production unless face marking of stones enabled any backlog to be tallied up

[6] Turner, A. J. 1948

once they were mortared into place. Workers may have been paid cash in hand for stones that were already on the bench. In this case there would have been no need to apply a mark as no record needed to be kept[7].

An alternative explanation might be that some workers were accustomed to marking their stones with lime or dye rather than the chisel. It is clear from existing literature on the subject that there were different working practices in different parts of the country that may have been reflected on a single building site where many diverse teams came together. Perhaps stone-working practises from Anglo-Norman, Anglo-Saxon and even Gaelic cultures came together on the 12th century Scottish building sites. Finally, some local workers may have cut stones as part of their feudal or kindred obligations rather than for cash payment as must have been the case with incomers.

Much more research needs to be carried out comparing the Scottish data to similar work in northern England. For example, is the apparent lack of banker marks at St Rule's due to the importation of Yorkshire working practices where marks were used sparingly? Does the profusion of marks at Markinch, Leuchars, Dalmeny and Legerwood point to a Durham or a Dunfermline connection? (this would indicate a different regional origin for the workmen at Markinch and St Rule's towers despite the superficial similarity of the buildings). Was there an expansion of the workforce north into Scotland after the downturn in building at Durham during the early 12th century or when the big project was finished? A better analysis of marks at Durham would help answer all these questions. Does the use of marks on a building signify a secular rather than an ecclesiastical patronage?

Conclusion

This comparative survey has been difficult to interpret, and it is impossible to date, even approximately, any of the buildings examined in the section with reference to the marks. It might, however, be tentatively suggested that the relative simplicity of the marks at Markinch and the lack of letters with serifs indicates that the building is earlier whilst the reverse is

[7] Thanks to Donald Mckenzie for this suggestion

true with respect to Dalmeny. In addition, each building would seem to have two types of marks ;-

1. temporary marks primarily used for purposes of identity and linked to piecework payment. These may have been allocated by the master mason specifically for the job or agreed amongst the workers themselves.

2. Personal marks brought to the job perhaps by more highly skilled workers . As well as securing payment these might have been intended to have additional functions including quality assurance, status display and possibly, in cases where letters were used, as a mark of basic literacy.

Markinch would appear to have more of the former category and Dalmeny more of the latter, Leuchars being somewhere in between.

If we accept that Dalmeny is later than Markinch then it seems to give us a clue as to how the marking system was developing, at least in eastern Scotland, during the 12th century. The copious use of letters with tags or serifs is either an indication of rank within the work community or a way of differentiating between different members of a team who use the same mark.

Perhaps marking systems in place during the 12th century differed from later medieval practice and we are seeing a snapshot of a set of working practices in transition. The marking of stones for payment was a highly practical arrangement and would have varied greatly according to the circumstances on any particular site but there may have been general trends within a particular region that can be identified.

Despite all the difficulties of interpretation, the picture beginning to emerge is of a competitive church building by secular and ecclesiastical rivals throughout eastern Scotland. This was carried out by teams of highly skilled workers assembled for each contract, supplemented by a number of workers moving from one site to another on short or day payment contracts. Local serfs or bondsmen trained on the job would have complicated the picture. New technology would have been imported and new local skills developed. The mark by a senior mason on the wall of Markinch church tower showing how the half-bonded stone building system should work has perhaps as much significance as an early charter. This would have set a clear standard for others to follow.

As regards the marking system, it was probably fluid and evolving rather than specific to individuals as it later became. There would perhaps have been "companies" with their own mark, family groups and individuals with apprentices. Different regional practices would probably come together on one site. Whatever system or systems were employed they are likely to have been highly pragmatic although features such as individual pride in workmanship, faith and superstition must have played their part.

Tagging systems may have been employed but equally human nature may have been reflected in the selection of marks, with a conservative approach being taken by some who recycled marks they had seen elsewhere, to a more radical and inventive approach to mark-creation as we see with the unique double arrow mark at Markinch cutting boldly across the stone from corner to corner. Similarities between marks might indicate family relationships but they might equally indicate carelessness by the mason after a hard day's work or a mistake by a team member unfamiliar with cutting the mark.

There would of course have been many more buildings constructed in Scotland during the 12th century than is apparent from today's vestiges. Most have been destroyed or drastically altered during the Reformation and in subsequent centuries. The marks selected for this analysis only provide a limited snapshot of all the marks that ever existed throughout the region. The pattern of marks on the few buildings that survive point to a complex set of working practices and patterns of itinerant employment that are only beginning to be understood. In the case of Markinch they have helped us understand the seasonal progress of building but have been less helpful with respect to dating.   However, the fact that the study has been able to "fingerprint" the stone cutting technique of at least one and possibly two individual masons holds out hope for future studies.

Many academics tend to overlook masons' marks but this small study concludes that the recording and study of banker marks in their proper context can contribute towards our understanding of the history and archaeology of Scotland's early buildings. If sufficient data is collected and sufficient attention is paid to detail, particularly for a single historical period, then patterns will emerge and, as with code breaking, exceptional events will point to underlying behaviour patterns giving an insight into working practices. Perhaps most importantly of all, the focus upon marks and building techniques shines a light on a stratum of society that the written record often overlooks.

Chapter 7

7. Who built the tower?
Bishop, Prior, Earl or Chieftain?

It was the height of summer when Bishop David de Bernham crossed the Leven and headed up the hill towards Markinch Church, The year was 1243 and it was the fourteenth day before the Kalends of August, that is the 19th of July. He and his group of monks had ridden from Largo where he had officiated at a church dedication the day before. We know this because of a small manuscript, rebound in red sharkskin, still preserved in the Bibliothèque Nationale de Paris. This document, in a 13th century script, records a remarkable series of journeys made by the Bishop during which he dedicated around 140 churches in his St Andrews diocese throughout Scotland. During his travels he used the words of dedication recorded in the manuscript as well as stanzas of plainsong as the book also contains musical notation[1]. Bound into the book is a list of the churches that he visited or rededicated.

He had visited Kinglassie a few weeks earlier but had continued down the Lochty Burn towards Scoonie, bypassing Markinch and heading straight for a dedication in St Andrews where he would have stayed during the festivities of Pentecost, falling on 31st of May that year. Almost three weeks later e set off along the coast again with the itinerary showing that he spent up to two weeks near Kilconquhar, perhaps lodging and negotiating with the Earl whose domain we believe was close by. He arrived at Markinch during the third week of July. We learn from a separate source[2] that he chose St John the Baptist to strengthen Markinch's sanctity, and the saints days of both St Drostan and St John were celebrated in Markinch down to the 19th century. Such a major reform may well have engendered resentment with a very traditionally minded local population although by 1243 the old priory on Loch Leven (Céli Dé) had been transformed and subsumed within the new Augustinian order.

---

[1] Wordsworth, C. (1885) The Pontifical Offices used by David de Bernham

[2] St A Lib 348 also Churches and saints listed together by Lockart, Rev. W. 1886 PSAS

Table 1	Kings of Scotland	Bishops of St Andrews	MacDuff Earls of Fife	MacDuff Clan Chiefs & heirs	Key Events in Fife
1050	MacBeth (1040-1057) Lu Malcolm III (1058⟶	Máel Dúin Túathal			Markinch Church and lands granted to Loch Leven Pr. (c 1050)
1060		Fothad II			
1070					
1080					
1090	Malcolm III (dies 1093) Donald III (1093-1097) Duncan II (1094) Edgar (1097-1107)	Girlc Cathroe	Constantine Earl (1095….)	Constantine Earl (1095….)	
1100	Alexander I (1107⟶)	Thurgot (1107-1115)			
1110	Q. Matilda (dies 1118)				(c1100 Auchmuir granted to Loch Leven
1120	Alexander I (dies 1124) David I (1124⟶)	Eadmer Robert (1124⟶)			-Kirkness marches dispute (c 1128) -Brieve re coop. with Dunf. (1124x1128) - Dunf. begun (1128)
1130			Constantine (dies c 1133) Gillemichael Earl (1133-1136) Duncan I Earl (1136 ⟶)	Gillemichael Earl (1133-1136)	(1128x1136) Kirkcaldy shire restored to Dunf. Abbey by David I
1140				?	North Berwick nunnery founded by Duncan I (c1150)
1150	David I (dies 1154) Malcolm IV (1154⟶)	Robert (dies 1159)	Duncan I (dies 1154) Duncan II Earl (1154 ⟶) (minor) CHURCH DONOR	Aedh I (Hugh son of Gillemichael) (1154-c1160 'regent' until Duncan II comes of age	-Cain of Markinch Church granted to St A's Priory by Robert (c1153) -Duncan II marries (c1160)
1160	Malcolm IV (dies 1165) William I (1165….)	Ernald (1160-63) Richard (1163⟶) CHURCH DONOR		Aedh II (Hugh son of Aedh I) CHURCH DONOR	-Markinch Ch. granted to St A's Priory by Bishop Richard, Duncan II & Aedh II (1165x1169))
1170		Richard (dies 1178) Hugh (1178⟶)			
1180		Hugh (dies 1188) Roger (1188⟶)			
1190					
1200		Roger (dies 1202) William (1202⟶)	Duncan II (dies 1204) Malcolm I Earl (1204….)	?	
1210	William I (dies 1214) Alexander II (1214⟶)				1217 - Founding of Culross Abbey by Malcom I
1220			Malcolm I (dies 1229) Malcolm II becomes earl	?	Gift of toft and one acre to Ch.by Malcolm
1230		William (dies 1238)			
1240		David de Bernham (1239-1253)			-1240 Markinch Ch. secured by Priory -1243 Rededication

The surviving record includes the services of dedication that Bishop David used on his tour. It was evidently an impressive and elaborate dedication that brought Markinch into the mainstream of Western Christianity, as Bishop David would have seen it.

We can safely assume from its style that Markinch tower as we know it today was built by 1243, and had been standing perhaps for over a century, but no record of its construction date remains. This chapter examines some of the likely patrons who may have built the church in an attempt to narrow down the possible dates. Table 1 sets out, alongside the Scottish monarchs, the key figures who are likely to have had a role in the

building of the church. Those who formally donated the church to St Andrews Priory in the 1160s are marked in red but as we go on to discuss, Bishop Robert made a gift of some minor church revenue from Markinch in the early 1150s (marked in green). A more detailed table of events impinging on Markinch's history during the 12th and early 13th centuries is set out at the end of the chapter.

Given the scarcity of evidence for the period[3] it will be necessary to examine means, opportunity and motive for each potential builder in turn. As we have demonstrated the physical connection between the tower and nave, the question of who built the tower also relates to the rest of the building. Sadly, there is no foundation charter or any indication of the movement of men and materials that would have been needed for such a major project. The copies of charters kept by the Priory of St Andrews were specifically selected to show proof of ownership. They were not set out as a chronicle and show no interest whatsoever in the history of the building or its construction. If such documents existed they may have been taken away or destroyed when Edward I encamped at Markinch in 1296 or, perhaps as likely, mouldered away in some garret of a prominent Fife family descended from the MacDuffs. The documents of Dunfermline Priory (later Abbey) are more of a chronicle and point to an ongoing series of disputes over what the priory considered was theirs by grant of King David and what the ruling families of Fife considered to be traditionally theirs. The records certainly point to competition over resources in Western Fife in the late 1120s but whether this hints at an underlying struggle between two competing building projects is

---

[3] for an overview see Oram, R. 2011 Domination and Lordship Scotland 1070 - 1230 pp. 378-9

impossible to judge. The MacDuffs found themselves under pressure from two different directions, the abbots of Dunfermline and the Bishops of St Andrews, but the earls seem to have been able to break out by establishing a

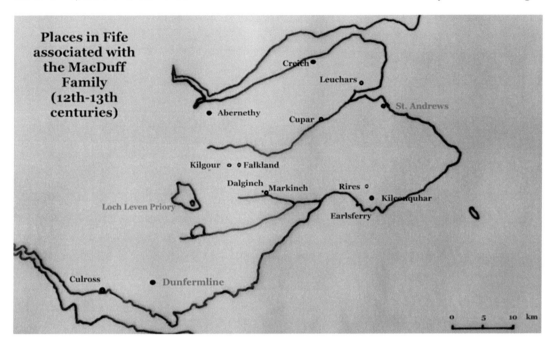

network of landowning interests across the whole of Scotland. Fortunately, recent writings have added considerably to our knowledge of this important Scottish family[4].

By the time Bishop de Bernham dedicated Markinch to St John the Baptist it was safely in the hands of the Priory of St Andrews after a long process that had lasted about one hundred years, beginning when David I decided to transfer ownership of Loch Leven Priory and its possessions from the Céli Dé monks to a newly created Priory based in St Andrews. By 1243 there had been six or seven priors of St Andrews since it was founded in the 1140s and on various occasions the property of the church or the church itself had been gifted or confirmed to the Priory but it was not until 1240 that they got the full use of the revenues linked to the church.

Church sponsored building activity?

We might begin our search for a builder with the churchmen of the 12th century, represented by the Abbots and Priors of Loch Leven Priory, the

---

[4] Both chapter and tables draw upon.Taylor, Dr Simon with Márkus, G. Place-Names of Fife Vols II and V (PNF II & V)

Bishops of St Andrews and the Augustinian Priors of St Andrews Priory, founded by David I around 1140. All three institutions had leaders that were known to have embarked upon construction projects from the late 11th up until the latter decades of the 12th century, and we must assume that most of their projects had the backing of the king with all the resources that such a relationship provided.

The circumstances surrounding the construction of the small chapel on St Serf's Inch on Loch Leven are obscure but collaboration between an Abbot and the Royal household residing at nearby Dunfermline would have been most likely. Could this small Priory have been responsible for the construction a "daughter church" at Markinch? A church of some description was gifted to the monks on the island by the bishop of St Andrews as early as the middle of the 11th century. Might the monks have reconstructed it on a grander scale some years later?

The probability is extremely low for two main reasons. Firstly, the resources available to the monks in terms of tiends and offerings was slender. We know this because the sum total of their possessions was enumerated and transferred to a newly created Priory in St Andrews around 1140. Secondly, the focus of any building activity would almost certainly have been on their own island and nearby possessions. Markinch had no particular significance to them other than a source of revenue. That is not to say that the monks had no interest in the building at all and there may be features of the design that were influenced by their traditions. The possible significance of the lozenge design has already been alluded to but if the church was decorated inside the designs may well have reflected traditional interpretations of biblical narratives.

If the monks of St Serf's were not the builders, might a bishop of St Andrews have initiated the construction? Several bishops may have had access to the necessary resources. These range from from Bishop Thurgot in the early part of the 12th century through to Bishop Robert who died in 1159 shortly before the church was gifted to the new Priory. However, none of them had a link to Markinch strong enough to justify the construction of such a high quality building. Robert was bishop for more than three decades, 1124/27 until his death in 1158/59. As David I's principal bishop, the building projects that he was involved in are well known - Scone (as Prior in 1120), Holyrood (1128), Stirling Cambuskenneth (c1140) and possibly St Regulus in

St Andrews. To participate in a building such as Markinch church, however, Robert needed a very close working relationship with the MacDuff family, local Markinch landowners closely connected to the place of legal assembly at Dalginch. From what little we know of the relationship between the MacDuffs and the church authorities in St Andrews, this seems unlikely. Robert, as Scotland's premier bishop, had a national role to fulfil and that did not include working alongside a Fife family, however exalted, in a location that had no particular significance for the national church. Markinch church tower, despite some similarities with St Rules tower, cannot be seen as part of a daughter church of the St Andrews Priory. In fact, if Robert was responsible for the construction of St Rules, he may have deliberately chosen the dimensions to dwarf the standing tower at Markinch. This seems more plausible than a powerful earl deliberately producing a smaller version of St Rules as has sometimes been suggested. The two buildings came under the ownership of St Andrews Priory much later in the 12th century as the result of a co-ordinated donation as we shall see later.

Clearly, Bishop Robert recognised that he had a historical claim linked to Markinch church (or part of it) when he transferred its revenues from the old priory to the new priory around 1153. As well as carrying out King David's wishes following his transfer of the Island on Loch Leven to the new Priory, Robert had a special affinity with the first prior, also called Robert, who passed through the same Yorkshire priory of Nostell. Although the charter is scrupulous in listing for transfer a number of properties including Kirkton of Scoonie, the actual church of Markinch and and its kirkton is not listed, only some revenue, set out in the charter as "20 cheeses and a pig from Markinch". This could of course express the vague nature of the rights surrounding a church but the charter distinguishes property from revenue and is explicit in so many other respects that we are inclined to think that these offerings were only part of a much wider picture now lost to us. Could it be that the church and land (or at least the major part of it) at that time were under the power of someone else, most probably the Earl or one of his kinsmen?

The date of the original transaction by Robert is not exact but Simon Taylor reckons it to be around 1153 at a time when David was donating St Serf's Inch itself to the new Priory. These donations of the Loch Leven Priory's possessions would have taken place either just before or during a series of major political upheavals. In rapid succession David I's heir to the throne, Henry died (1152). Perhaps sensing that his own end was near David secured the services of Duncan II Earl of Fife to escort his young grandson and newly appointed heir around the realm. This would have emphasised to the Gaelic lords of Scotland that the principal of primogeniture would be the rule of the realm. David himself died shortly afterwards (1153), leaving his grandson Malcolm (IV) to inherit the throne as a minor. Earl Duncan might well have become regent given his former close working relationship with the young Malcolm but within a short time Duncan too was dead (1154). His heir as earl, Duncan II inherited the earldom as a child and the position at the head of the Scottish nobility appears to have been given to the next senior earl, Ferteth of Strathearn. The affairs of the earldom were managed by the MacDuff clan chief, a theme developed further below. Perhaps Bishop Robert had tried to reach an agreement with the MacDuff family over a joint donation of Markinch church and its property but had failed. Perhaps the dynastic upheavals of the time intervened. If Robert had intended his gift of the pig and the cheeses to have prompted the secular powers into parting with more substantial land and property from Markinch then, for whatever reason, he was unsuccessful and the matter was shelved for half a generation until king, earl and even bishop had been replaced.

The most likely explanation is that a church building existed at that troubled time, constructed not by the bishop but by a member of the MacDuff family. The bishop had certain historical rights but they were not complete and not absolute. If that church had been the same one granted to the Loch Leven monks by the bishop of St Andrews in the 1050s then surely Bishop Robert would have included it in its entirety in the bundle of properties and revenues seized for the new Priory. A reasonable conclusion would therefore be that the church was built by a secular power before 1153 but that the ecclesiastical power retained certain historical rights that were divested at the king's behest.

No mention of Markinch church or its revenues is made by Robert's successor Ernald during his short episcopacy (1160-63) and his focus was probably upon the possessions of the Bishopric rather than the Priory. A charter, probably drawn up at the time of his inauguration in 1160, lists much property of the church but makes no mention of any of the Priory's

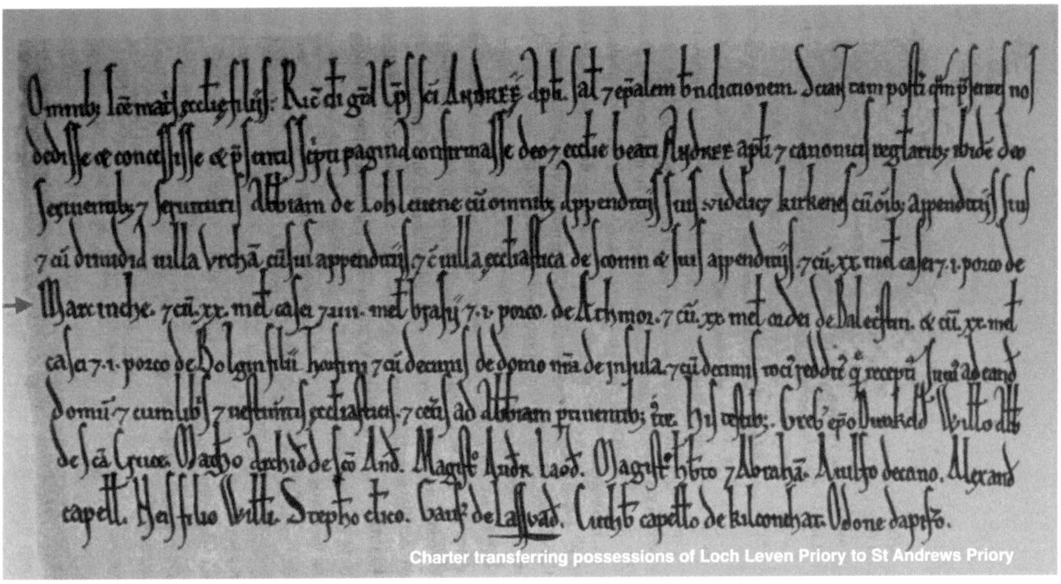

Charter transferring possessions of Loch Leven Priory to St Andrews Priory

possessions including Markinch.[5] It is witnessed by a host of clerics as well as Duncan II Earl of Fife, Ness son of William and Orm the son of Hugo, all members of the MacDuff family. Ernald is believed to have laid the foundations for St Andrews Cathedral and would have had little interest in building in a relatively remote village such as Markinch. The same could not be said for the members of the MacDuff family who witnessed his first charter.

Richard, his successor as bishop continued with the cathedral building project and went to some lengths to confirm the transfer of property and revenues from Loch Leven.   This included the cheeses and the pig from Markinch (the illustration below is a copy of his confirmation charter, *St A Lib 175*). However, he subsequently seems to have been part of a joint donation of Markinch church and its Kirkton alongside two prominent members of the MacDuff family in the latter part of the 1160s. This is developed more fully in the later section dealing with the three donors. The language of his charters changes from revenue to buildings and land once the MacDuff family become part of the joint enterprise. Richard, like his predecessor, and indeed his successors, would have had no motivation to build so far from the focus of his episcopacy in St Andrews where a new cathedral required all the resources that could be mustered until the end of the century and beyond. The focus was upon revenue and an 1166 joint

---

[5] St A Lib 130

donation of "Markinch Church with all its possessions" was probably much more lucrative than the 1153 donation of "twenty cheeses and a pig". A taxation list drawn up a century later[6] shows that Markinch Church was valued at a higher level than any other church in the diocese except Dunfermline and Greater Kinghorn, although all three may have been enriched by pilgrim traffic.

Neither are any of the new priors of St Andrews likely to have had anything to do with the building project at Markinch. Throughout the second half of the 12th century their building focus would have been on their own Priory just as it had been for the Abbots on Loch Leven in earlier years. Markinch for bishops, priors and abbots alike was another potential revenue stream but it probably took many years for the revenue to flow despite the wording of the charters. Some of the revenue in the gift of the bishop may well have been transferred to them in 1153 but it was probably not until the 1240s before full patronage and other sources of revenue, linked to the church but under the control of the MacDuffs, was released. With it would come full patronage and the right to make appointments.

Any incentive to construct in a location such as Markinch would have been linked to its status as a place of justice, and that points to the secular authorities, the MacDuffs, as secular sponsors and patrons. Markinch was in close proximity to Dalginch where successive earls or their representatives adjudicated, probably in open air trials. A suitably prestigious place to hold mass either before or after a trial would have been essential. Family members would have been buried under and around the church.

It has been well argued by Bannerman that there were two intermingling lines of succession amongst the MacDuffs in early medieval Fife[7]. To simplify, the earls traced descent through a system of primogeniture first established by King David I and introduced when Earl Duncan I fell heir to his father Constantine, the first earl for whom we have records. On the other hand the MacDuff clan chieftainship continued a process characterised by an ancient *tànaiste* succession whereby the ablest kinsman of a generation stepped into the leadership role, usually by acclaim or by kinship. Bannerman shows how in the feudal period when an earl was too young to be an effective leader, a

[6] St A Lib 29

[7] Bannerman, J. in Grant, A. and Stringer, K. J. *Medieval Scotland* (1998)

chief styled MacDuff came to the fore. As we shall see, the secular donors, of the late 1160s, Duncan II and Aedh II, both members of different branches of the MacDuff family, represented the two lines of succession, earl and clan chief.

If we are to seek a builder for Markinch Church then it is to the powerful MacDuff family that we must turn, a family linked by tradition to the place of justice near Markinch. As the building of the church has been given a wide range of dates by successive writers, we begin in the early 13th century with the most recent candidate and work back in time.

Earl Malcolm and his Nephew - 13th Century Builders?

In terms of secular authority, the MacDuff Earl of Fife in 1243 when Markinch was rededicated was Malcolm II, the nephew of Malcolm I. According to Sibbald, he or possibly his uncle had a castle at Brunton (Dalginch) by Markinch but this is most unlikely to have been his principal place of residence. The area has not yet been excavated but there are no obvious signs of tooled stone, although these may have been incorporated into Brunton House which was largely removed in the late 1960s. If Malcolm II ever had any charters relating to Markinch they are no longer in existence and the impression from those few charters that remain is of a man more concerned with international affairs and his uncle's abbey at Culross. He would, however, have been aware that his grandfather had donated Markinch Church to the St Andrews Priory in 1165-66. If Malcolm had built Markinch church then the donation would surely have been recorded in the Cartulary of St Andrews Priory.

A similar argument holds for his uncle and predecessor Malcolm I who assumed the earldom in 1204, no doubt in the full knowledge that Markinch Church had already been donated to the Priory in 1165-66. He is thought responsible for the gift of some land next to the church cemetery, possibly to build lodgings for the Prior but his building focus would have been on Culross which he is thought to have founded in 1217.[8]

---

[8] St A Lib 245

We can conclude therefore that there is little or no evidence that either churchman or secular landowner constructed the church as late as the 13th century and we now turn to the century before.

One Donation to the New Priory, three donors

According to several separate charters or charter confirmations, Markinch Church and its lands were gifted to the newly created Priory of St Andrews more than a decade after Bishop Robert had donated produce from the lands of the old church as part of the transfer of assets from St Serf's Isle. Dates of charters have to be estimated from known events at this period but it is safe to say that no less than three separate donors (marked in red in table 1) are identified in separate charters of around 1166, copies of which are bound within the pages of a property record kept by St Andrews Priory [9] :-

a) Bishop Richard of St Andrews,

b) Earl Duncan (II) of Fife (by now in his majority) and

c) Aedh (II), son of Aedh (I), son of Gillemichael, Earl of Fife

Closer inspection of the three documents reveals that Bishop Richard's donation was witnessed by churchmen and their household, whereas Earl Duncan's donation was witnessed by lay persons. Duncan's charter was addressed to all men, Scots, English and French and the witness list was headed by a woman, Countess Ela. This form of address perhaps emphasised to his new wife that Duncan was at ease amongst the multilingual Scottish aristocracy.

For three such eminent men to identify with the gift of the building and its pertinents suggests that it was by this time of some significance, but was the tower and nave newly built or, perhaps already several decades old? The fact that Richard's charter suggests an ecclesiastical sealing ceremony whereas Duncan's was transacted in a secular setting gives weight to the suggestion that the bishop's rights lay in part of the building such as the chancel whereas Duncan's right as a patron or principal heritor perhaps lay in the nave. The division could in reality have been much vaguer. Another charter confirming general rights over Loch Leven Abbey and its possessions was confirmed by Richard, probably on the same occasion as his Markinch charter, judging by

---

[9] see Taylor op. cit and Corpus of Scottish Medieval Parish Churches, School of Art History, University of St Andrews. The charters are respectively a) St A Lib 135, b) St A Lib 242 and c) St A Lib xxi

the similarity of the witness list[10]. Aedh's gift on the other hand is a marginal entry in the Liber. The witness list is headed by Bishop Robert but is shorter and less prestigious than the other two. Nevertheless, when King William later confirms the gift he refers to Aedh as the donor of both the church and a toft to the east an interesting point of detail suggesting local knowledge[11]. The parallel donation of Earl Duncan is not mentioned in this charter despite the fact that the confirmation is witnessed by both Aedh's brother and Duncan himself. This appears to reinforce the claim of Aedh's line traced back to Gillemichael over the claims of the earl's line traced back through Duncan I, although competition between the two lines is suggested by the fact that William draws up separate charter confirmations for the Earl (including a chapel at Kettle).[12]

It is evident that the principal individual responsible for the building's construction was either one of these three men or one of their predecessors. We have ruled out the involvement of Bishop Richard or any other churchman and so our attention must turn to the intermingling lines of the MacDuffs. The chapter sets out the case for each in turn, starting with the grantors referred to above and moving back in time to Constantine, the first known MacDuff earl of Fife.

In reality, despite the wording of the charters in the 1160s, the transfer process to the new Priory was long and protracted involving not only the church building but also associated land, revenue from the land and the right to appoint vicars. As already noted it was not until well into the 13th century that all aspects of Markinch Church, its lands and revenue and appointments of its clergy were firmly in the hands of the Priory. The process was intimately linked with an attempt to submerge the old Céli Dé monastic order followed by a renewed movement in the 13th century to transform and absorb it into the wider structure of the reformed church[13].

The grants appear on the surface to be about land, buildings and tiends but they also represent a process of reforming or uprooting an old form of religion sketched out by Thurgot in his Life of Margaret at the beginning of

[10] St A Lib 175

[11] St A Lib 213

[12] St A Lib 220 and St A Lib 230

[13] Barrow, G. W. S. The Kingdom of the Scots (2003)

the 12th century. Reform was a gradual process probably involving a struggle for hearts and minds, benefices and offices. As far as Markinch was concerned it was begun by Bishop Robert, who as we have seen was encouraged by David I, most probably in the early 1150s, shortly after the Priory of St Andrews was founded. It lasted many decades, with a pact between the Priory of St Andrews and the Bishop (surprisingly representing the interests of the Céli Dé) in the final years of the 12th century, witnessed by a wide selection of the powerful laymen of Fife[14]. However, as far as Markinch is concerned it did not really end until 1240. In that year several of Bishop de Bernham's household and various lay witnesses convened across the water from Fife in Tyninghame, East Lothian. The charter agreed at that meeting finally ensured that Markinch and Cupar churches were secured "in usus proprios" by the Priory.[15] Three years later Markinch church was rededicated by the same bishop, bestowing upon St Drostan's the new dedication of St John the Baptist.

The documents relating to Markinch that we now have copies of dating from 1150 to 1250 represent that long process of power transferring from the old order to the new. Markinch, as a former possession of the Island priory and probably under the protection of the powerful MacDuff family, was simply caught up in the process. The documents include no fewer than four papal confirmations[16] and the intervention of several Scottish monarchs. In focussing upon the replacement of the monks on the Island by Augustinians we should not overlook the many parish priests once dependent upon the old Abbey who must have clung on to their benefices perhaps supported by the local population or by local landowners. We do not know the relationship between the MacDuffs and the priests at Markinch during this difficult period of transition but we do know how close the family was to the cult of St Serf. Were the late 12th century vicars really appointees of the St Andrews Priory or were they in effect Céli Dé as in Streathearn for which we have better documentation? Might they have been family appointees placed in office in a way similar to the lay abbots of Abernethy? This privilege of preferment may explain why the process of transfer to the Priory took so long, with the

---

[14] St A. Lib. 318-319

[15] St A Lib 166

[16] Corpus of Scottish Medieval Parish Churches, St Andrews Univ.

MacDuff family retaining this vestige of a privilege long after the revenue and the building itself had been handed over.

By the middle of the 13th century, the MacDuff family had shifted its main focus of interest away from Markinch and its links with the old Priory. As we have seen, a new abbey had been built by Earl Malcolm I at Culross and so the Macduffs were themselves importing a new religious order following the lead of their monarchs. That abbey was, however, built over the remains of a Pictish church supposedly founded by St Serf himself. Markinch was firmly in the hands of the new Priory of St Andrews but at Culross the MacDuffs retained an old family connection to a saint[17].

Earl Duncan II (1154 - 1204) as Builder and Grantor?

Duncan II was earl from 1154 when he inherited the earldom during his childhood to 1204 when he died.

It is unlikely that the Duncan II undertook a building project in the 1150s. As noted he was in his minority when he acquired the earldom in 1153 and it seems that his affairs were being handled by MacDuff, the clan chief (identified by Bannerman as Aedh I, see below)[18]. This was an arrangement that was not unique during the MacDuff dynasty, a clan chief elected under the old rules acting as "regent" during the minority of a young earl inheriting the earldom by process of primogeniture. It is just as unlikely that he built the church after it had been donated to the priory and so a post 1166 date is ruled out.

Earl Duncan II was married to a close kinswoman of the deceased Malcolm IV around 1160 and inherited substantial territory around Falkland, Strathmiglo and Kingskettle along with his bride. Under these circumstances we might have expected a substantial building in Falkland or at nearby Kilgour but not at Markinch. Duncan's father, Earl Duncan I was key to securing the feudal framework of Scotland established by King Malcolm IV's grandfather David. Might a newly built church in the heart of the earl's

---

[17] for more on the links between St Serf and the MacDuff earls see Taylor, S. (2012) PNF Vol. 5

[18] Bannerman, J. in Grant, A. and Stringer, K. J. (1998)

ancestral territory drawing upon the king's own contacts have been part of a wedding settlement begun around 1160 when he married the king's close relative? If so, then given the date, we might have expected more remnants from inside the building of the kind of bold architectural detail displayed at Leuchars or Dalmeny rather than four pieces of very traditional chip-cut carving and a plain ashlar tower arch.

Duncan may well have continued to have links to Markinch during the latter years of the 12th century and there is a record of a charter being sealed at Markinch by the King's brother, the Earl of Huntingdon in 1171/72[19]. Earl Duncan II is one of the witnesses and the ceremony may well have taken place within the church or the tower.[20] If the group had been taking part in a hunting expedition, as the nature of the *reddendo* extracted from Longforgan suggests (a goshawk), then Markinch tower would have been an excellent vantage point.

It is therefore difficult to identify Duncan II's motive or his opportunity to build and it is most likely that he was merely gifting a building over which he had some sort of proprietorial claim either by direct inheritance or by inherited feudal superiority.

Aedh II (c1154 - c1165) as Builder and Grantor?

One of the three separate recorded donors of Markinch Church itself was Aedh II, or to give him the anglicised title used in his donation charter, "Hugo, son of Hugo, son of Gillemichael Earl of Fife". The only other time this name appears is in a charter confirmation by William I written a few years later where he is referred to as knight.[21] The donation, included in King William's general confirmation charter of 1165 x 1169, has a strong ring of authenticity about it as it refers to a piece of land or toft to the east of the church as well as the church itself. By contrast, Earl Duncan II's charter refers only in general terms to the church itself. This toft most probably was the vicar's plot immediately to the south of land that was later gifted to the new Priory by Earl Malcolm I. For some reason, the toft appears in the

---

[19] Stringer, K. J. The Acts of Earl David of Huntingdon. No 28 (pp 235-6)

[20] NLS Charter 7710

[21] St A Lib 213

confirmation but not in the original charter which refers simply to the property of the church in general. This may have been an insert at the behest of Aedh II's brother, Orm of Abernethy, who is one of the witnesses to the confirmation. Perhaps by the time of the confirmation the house and the surrounding plot of the vicar had become a contentious issue and the opportunity was taken to resolve it through the charter confirmation.

Simon Taylor points out that this branch of the MacDuffs was closely associated with Markinch.[22] Early in his reign King William confirmed an exchange of land for Aedh II's brother, Orm of Abernethy. Land at Balbirnie, close by Markinch Church, was exchanged for land at Glenduckie and Balmeadie (Dunbog Parish), thus consolidating Orm's Abernethy landholding as well as giving Earl Duncan more complete possession of his wider Strathleven feudal landholding (present day Markinch Parish).[23] Bannerman points out that Aedh I was clan chief during the minority of Duncan II (1154 - c1160). Aedh II was therefore the son of a MacDuff clan chief but there is no evidence that he held the title which may have been taken by Earl Duncan II himself when he came of age

It is strange that such an important member of the MacDuff family as Aedh II has so little charter evidence but we might suspect that he does appear elsewhere under a different guise, perhaps due to a transcription error as Aviel of Strathleven or even Hugh of Markinch, the Clerk of the earl.[24] A knight would certainly have a territory for his service and the earl of Fife may have already sub-feued Strathleven to a close kinsman who would have further sub-feued to territories within Strathleven such as Dalginch, Balbirnie and Markinch itself.

Such an identification will have to await further manuscript research but at the time of the donation, Aedh II would only recently have inherited his right in Markinch church presumably from his father Aedh I, son of Gillemichael. He would have had little opportunity to build a major church himself but could conceivably have completed one begun by his father. Alternatively, his interest in the church may have come from the fact that he sub-feued the land of Markinch or even the surrounding shire in its entirety.

[22] PNF II p. 394

[23] RRS ii No 14

[24]PoMS, no. 5638 (http://db.poms.ac.uk/record/person/5638/; accessed 26 March 2016)

There is of course the possibility that, like his brother Orm who had been installed as lay abbot of Abernethy, Aedh II had an ecclesiastical office such as Priest of Markinch church.

Aedh I (1154 - c1160) MacDuff Clan Chief as Builder?

Aedh II's father, Aedh I (Hugo son of Gillemichael) is a different proposition, however. If, as John Bannerman argues, the title of MacDuff had been given to Aedh I (anglicised as Hugh I), then it would have brought him great prestige amongst the Gaelic aristocracy. This would have been enhanced during the years from 1154 and c1160 when he looked after the affairs of the young earl Duncan II. It is also probable that, like his son Orm, he acquired the title of lay Abbot of Abernethy, perhaps as compensation for not assuming the earldom in the old Gaelic *tànaiste* way. He may even have drawn upon land revenues linked to his clan chieftainship status[25]. Would he, however, have had the audacity to construct such a prestigious project under the nose of the young earl who was, in a sense his ward? It could be argued that it was an act of bravado to show his kin that, although barred from the earldom himself by the newly introduced feudal rules, he was the son of an earl and worthy of such a prestigious building.

It would appear that Gillemichael, Aedh I's father had inherited the earldom in the old *tànaiste* way, by popular acclaim of his kinsmen but himself died a few years later. This provided King David I with the opportunity to assert upon Fife the principal of primogeniture whereby an eldest son inherited from his father. By recognising Duncan I, Constantine's son, as successor to Gillemichael rather than Gillemichael's offspring, David I, in effect, deprived Aedh I of the earldom in succession to his father Gillemichael. The compensation appears to have been the grant of the secular title Abbot of Abernethy to Gillemichael's line. Might we not, however, have expected any prestigious building project to have taken place in Abernethy where that branch of the family now had firm roots?

Aedh I certainly had the motive to build a prestige project to demonstrate his standing amongst the MacDuff kinship network but it is less clear that he

---

[25] Broun, D. *Origins of the Mormaer* in Broun, *Statehood and Lordship*

had either the means or the opportunity. Significant resources would have been required to build a large church of some quality and it is not clear that as guardian he commanded the resources of the earldom. Add to that the limited opportunity that he had between the time he took over the wardship in 1154 and Duncan II's coming of age around 1159 and he begins to look increasingly unlikely as a potential builder of Markinch church. This reinforces the conclusion that the building took place prior to 1154, but still leaves open the question as to why his son had such a strong claim to be associated with the joint donation of around 1166.

One final observation needs to be made before we leave the Aedhs, both father and son (or the Hugos as their alternative names were) . We have noted in our survey of the tower that the graffiti was carefully assessed as part of the project. One set at the very top of the tower beside a cross had the deeply incised initials **AP**. We will never know for sure when and upon whose

Cross and inscribed lettering

behalf these initials were carved but it is worth considering the possibility that one of the Aedh MacDuffs styled himself *Aedh Presbitero* or Hugh the Priest, having been given office in the "family" church, perhaps by the earl. We have noted already that the records[26] refer to a character sometimes known as Hugh the Clerk and sometimes as Hugh of Markinch. He is a witness to several charters in the fourth quarter of the 12th century. Might Hugh the Priest, or perhaps his son, have become Hugh the Clerk to the earl as the church, step by step was passing into the hands of the Priory? If so then this could have been an added factor delaying the final transfer *in usus proprios* to the Priory of St Andrews. Even if the above hypothesis is rejected it still seems more than likely that the MacDuffs throughout the 12th century held the privilege of selecting priests to perform service in their churches.

[26]PoMS, no. 5638 (http://db.poms.ac.uk/record/person/5638/; accessed 26 March 2016)

Duncan I (1136 - 1154) as Builder?

Moving back again in time, could the work have been that of the third recorded earl of Fife, Duncan I? Duncan I held the earldom from 1133 to 1154 inheriting it from his kinsman Earl Gillemichael but also in another sense from his presumed father Earl Constantine, Gillemichael's predecessor. His earldom lasted twenty one years and he was once believed to have been the first Scottish noble to have his territory re-granted to him by feudal charter[27]. Although the evidence for a formal feudal charter has recently been disputed[28] what little evidence remains suggests a close relationship with King David. It was he who conducted David's grandson Malcolm around Scotland confirming his legitimacy when David's only son Henry died in 1152. On the death of David the following year, Duncan ensured that the young king was safely on the throne before he too died.

Duncan had ample opportunity during a lengthy earldom to construct the church at Markinch and charter proof exists of his building activity. Duncan I was responsible for the construction of two hospices on either side of the Forth, no doubt part of a strategy to improve the travel links with England and to consolidate his presence in East Lothian.[29] He is certainly in the frame as a likely builder of Markinch Church, although we might expect his territorial interests to have been closer to MacDuff lands around Kilconquhar and Elie and to family lands in East Lothian than to an inland site such as Markinch.

One possible scenario is that Duncan I built the church in the 1130s or 1140s but poor relations with Bishop Robert or the confusion of succession around the year 1153 or even Duncan's own death in 1154 prevented a joint donation to St Andrews Priory. Robert went ahead with his part of the arrangement, the "cheese and the pig", but the Earl, the principal patron of the church, never completed the joint donation. Another scenario is that Robert attempted to effect a joint donation earlier in Duncan's earldom but

---

[27] Barrow, G. W. S. (1980) *The Anglo Norman Era in Scottish History* p 35

[28] Taylor, Alice (2016) pp 51-52

[29] North Berwick Cartulary 4-5

agreement could not be reached. Some evidence exists of tension between what we now believe to have been Duncan's father Constantine and Bishop Robert with both turning up to an adjudication at the head of their respective armed contingents around 1128. The judgement went in favour of the Céli Dé, and Constantine is praised for his prudence. Perhaps some of this hostility passed over to his successor earl Duncan. What we can be sure of is that all parties at this time were motivated by guilt, fear of illness and impending death.

As Duncan I's son was in his minority when his father died, Robert found that he had to contend with Aedh I, a traditional MacDuff clan chief, and no further progress on the donation was made until both Robert and Aedh I were dead some fourteen or so years later, the tripartite donation being made by the successors to Duncan I, Aedh I and Bishop Robert.

A church with a tower built by Duncan in the 1130s or 1140s would inevitably have been compared with the standing church of St Rules a mere twenty miles away at St Andrews. Duncan was the senior member of the Scottish nobility, probably a Justiciar of Scotland and sufficiently close to King David to be entrusted as *rector* of the young Malcolm. He would have considered himself to have been at least on an equal footing with Bishop Robert. Under these circumstances we have to ask whether he would have a built a church for himself that was to all appearances a scaled down version of Robert's great monument at St Andrews.

We must also ask why a reference to an ownership claim by Aedh II, the son of a MacDuff clan chief, be inserted into a charter drawn up by a recently crowned William I in the late 1160s? Why indeed should a separate donation charter gifting Markinch Church to the Priory exist alongside one drawn up by the Earl? One possibility is that the two secular donors of 1165-66, Duncan II and Aedh II both derived their legitimacy to make the gift from a single individual who was himself responsible for the building of Markinch Church and he and his predecessor are considered next taking us into the earlier years of the century.

Gillemichael (c1133 - 1136) Earl and Clan Chief as Builder?

Aedh I's father Gillemichael seems to have been both Clan Chief and Earl before David granted the Earldom to Duncan I. Might Aedh II's grandfather Gillemichael, actually referred to in the charter of the c1166, have been our builder? It is he who appears in many of the 19th century antiquarian books as the traditional founder of the church, sometimes citing local tradition. His earldom was relatively short, probably three and no more than six years, hardly enough time to even raise the necessary funds, assemble the workforce and dig the foundations. Opportunity may well have been lacking but it is just possible that he finished a building begun by a predecessor or began a project completed by his successor.

Constantine (c1195 - c1133) Earl and Clan Chief as Builder?

His predecessor as earl was Constantine (Caustantin), both earl and clan chief from the mid 1090s until his death around 1133. He was the senior noble in Scotland, descended from a royal lineage as well as being the highest ranking lawman certainly north of the Forth.[30] As a senior judge, the prestige of his place of legal assembly would have been important to him. He was also the noble who had the right to crown the king and probably led the Scottish army at some point during his time as earl. With an earldom lasting over thirty five years one would assume that he had the opportunity and the resources to command a building of the highest standard, perhaps even innovative in style or modelled upon buildings well beyond the realm. Roger of Sarum was Justiciar of England for a period spanning part of Constantine's earldom. His power and influence within the legal system led him to amass great wealth and he was a major builder throughout England. Originally a priest from Avranche near Caen in Normandy he would have had access to master builders and masons of the highest order. We do not know, however, whether he ever met up with his Scottish counterpart and any transmission of ideas and manpower between the two must remain speculative.

---

[30] Barrow, G. W. S. *The Justiciar* in The Kingdom of the Scots

We must also remember the close relations between Scotland and the lands of Cumbria, Northumberland and Durham. Alexander, later king, is recorded in the *Liber Vitae* as being present at Durham during the translation of St Cuthbert's relics, a saint revered throughout southern Scotland and Northern England. It is reasonable to assume that his premier earl could have made similar visits. Additionally, if Constantine was Justiciar of Scotland then this must have brought him into close contact with the Royal Court opening up the possibility of contact with southern England and Normandy. From what little we know about Constantine his power seems to be based upon kinship ties as well as disposable wealth derived perhaps from his legal status within Scotland. He may have been able to secure a large unskilled workforce and have the wealth to import the skills needed for a complex building.

The undocumented relationship between an ageing Constantine and a young David I after 1124 would have been crucial in terms of David's struggle to secure Scotland during the early part of David's reign. Constantine would most probably have had an awareness of building styles through Thurgot, Prior of Durham and Bishop of St Andrews. He may have thrown his lot in behind David as he had with David's royal brothers in a shrewd calculation of the strength of competing forces. David may have been indebted to Constantine as the king struggled to control the country during the early years of his monarchy. As Clan Chief Constantine may have ensured that his MacDuff kinsmen fought for David against the rebellious forces in the North. The provision of a royal master mason for Markinch church could well have been part of his reward, in which case we would look to possible master masons familiar to the higher echelons of the English church and workmen from Huntingdon or Durham which was undergoing a lull in construction activity during the 1120s.

The flattering comments about Constantine made in the records of the monks of St Serf's relate to his efforts to secure their land in the face of an Anglo-Norman landowner but the old order of monks may also have expected him to defend their interests in the face of incoming ecclesiastical appointments from the South. The question then arises if Constantine was the builder of the new church, to whom would he have turned for permission to demolish the old church that had been granted to these monks in the middle of the 11th century. Was permission from the Prior of St Serf's Inch sufficient or would the Bishop of St Andrews have had to give his approval as well? It may have been that the wrangle over Bishop Robert's consecration between 1124 and 1127[31] was the opportunity for Constantine to take the initiative and make a start to the building project in the years immediately before his death. This would have meant that when Robert later in the 1130s came under pressure from King David to hand over the old Priory's possessions to the new Augustinian Order in St Andrews, the bishop had nothing at Markinch to transfer except the revenue from the old church. Anything more in terms of an actual building or even its patronage would by then have required the permission of the earl as secular patron, and as we know from the above discussion this was not forthcoming until the 1160s.

Constantine like his successors must have felt himself under ecclesiastical pressure from two separate directions, St Andrews and Dunfermline. There is a document[32] written between 1125 and 1128 that hints at a struggle over human resources between the monastery in Dunfermline and a man also by the name of Constantine that was possibly a member of the Earl's kin group. A king's brieve orders him not to withhold labour from the monastery. It would not have been surprising if Earl Constantine himself had withheld skilled men from King David's great project, particularly if he had an ongoing project of his own at Markinch. Tension over whether men and families belonged to the earl or the abbot continued for many decades[33]. Given the implied importance of these men to successive abbots and earls it is to be wondered whether they were simple serfs or had specific skills relevant to a building project such as wrights, masons or quarrymen.

Of course if the building of the church pre-dates the installation of Robert in 1123/24 then we have to examine the relationship between Constantine, King Alexander and Thurgot who was bishop between 1107 and 1115. Thurgot was both prior and archdeacon at Durham in the last decade of the 11th century. Alas the records for Scotland during this early period are almost non-existent. At that time the building of the great cathedral was just beginning at Durham but Thurgot would have been familiar with its predecessor, the *ecclesia major,* a stone church with Anglo-saxon roots but one for which no image survives. A high quality church building of this

---

[31] Oram, R. (2011) Domination and Lordship, Scotland 1070 - 1230

[32] Charters, David I No. 17 (1124 x i128)

[33] See Taylor (2012) Appendix 1 on the genealogies of the men of Dunfermline Abbey.

period could well have had the technical sophistication of Anglo-Norman building practices but contain aesthetic elements derived from the Anglo-Saxon world.

Conclusion

To sum up, there is no evidence to point to an ecclesiastical builder of Markinch Church although it is possible that the Bishop of St Andrews preserved certain rights as a result of his historical stake in the old church building that it is believed once occupied the site. A church built by an earl in the 13th century or even the late 12th century is extremely unlikely. Neither is there any single piece of incontrovertible evidence that attributes the building process to any of the names mentioned in the charters of around 1166 although it is more likely that it was an ancestor or predecessor of either Earl Duncan II or Aedh II rather than either of the men themselves or their descendants.

A building date between 1154 and c1160 would point to Aedh I, the MacDuff clan chief displaying his lineage to his kinsmen during the minority of Duncan II. It is possible that a kinsman of the young Earl Duncan II, styled MacDuff, constructed the church whilst he had wardship between 1154 and c1160 but it is unlikely that such a daring act could be completed in so short a time, particularly if extensive foundations had to be laid involving the transportation of sand and clay.

If the building was constructed between 1133 and 1153 it would suggest Duncan I as builder, perhaps in the 1140s when King David was setting him up as a model feudal leader but we find no evidence of cooperation with Bishop Robert during this period. If we are to accept Duncan I as the builder then we still have to account for Aedh II's strong interest in the building around 1166 when the major donation to St Andrew's Priory took place. It is speculated this may relate to Aedh's incumbency within the church during the late 1160s as a secular priest but we have no direct evidence for that.

Finally, a building date prior to 1133 implicates Constantine, perhaps constructing the building in the late 1120s, and dying before it was finished, leaving his successor Gillemichael to consecrate it in the mid 1130s. As the senior Scottish lawman, Constantine would have ample opportunity to build

Table 2	Key Dates relevant to Markinch Church (post 1120). Source : PNF II & V
1120	1124 King Alexander I dies 1124 David I inaugurated 1124 x 1128 Brieve commanding men to cooperate with work of building Dunfermline Church (ST Vol V)
1130	1128 x 1136 David I grants Kirkcaldy Shire to Dunfermline Abbey (held forcibly by Constantine) (PNF Vol V)
1140	1140 - St Andrews Augustinian priory founded by David I 1141 Future Malcolm IV born
1150	c1150 Duncan I builds nunnery at North Berwick 1152-53 David I donates St Serf's Inch to St A's Priory (ST vol II) 1152-53 Bishop Robert grants Abbey of Lochleven (+ everything belonging to it) to St A's Priory 1153 ? (est by S.Taylor) Markinch *cain* (pig and cheeses) granted to St A's Priory 1152 (12th Jun) Earl Henry dies 1152-53 Procession around Scotland by Duncan I and future Malcolm IV 1153 (May 24) David I dies 1153 (27th May) Malcolm IV accedes as minor to throne 1154 Duncan I Earl of Fife dies (succeeded by Ferteth as premier earl of Scotland) 1154 Duncan II succeeds as minor to Earldom Fife. 1153 x 1162 Hugh I (Aedh I) (MacDuff) & Duncan I or II addressed in brieve by Malcolm IV re Dunfermline and taking of conveth 1158-59 Bishop Robert dies 1159 Earl Duncan II witnesses first charter
1160	1160 (-62) Bishop Ernald inaug. 1161 - St Andrews cathedral begun 1160 (25th Dec.) Duncan II marries Ada (Ela/Hela/Adela) close relative of Malcolm IV 1162 Malcolm IV aged 21 years 1160 x 1162 King Malcolm IV grants Duncan II Falkland, Kingskettle, etc 1162 Bishop Ernald dies 1163 (-78) Bishop Richard the Chaplain inaug. 1163 Duncan II head of comital list of witnesses for the first time (adult) 1164 x 66 Bishop Richard (re)grants Lochleven Abbey (incl Markinch with its Kirkton) to St. A's Priory (ST Vol II) 1165 x 72 Lands at Tough and Bogie granted to MacDuff (Aedh II?) 1165-66 Bishop Richard Grants Markinch Church with everything belonging to it to St A's Priory (ST Vol II) 1165-66 Duncan II grants Markinch Church (with everything belonging to it) to St A's Priory (ST Vol II) 1165 x 1169 King William confirms grant of knight Aedh II, son of Aedh I son of Gillemichael of Markinch Church with toft on east side to St A's Priory (Witnessed by Abbot Orm brother of Aedh II)
1170	1165 X 1171 William confirms exchange of Balbirnie and Glenduckie etc between Abbot Orm and Duncan II 1165 X 1171 William I grants Strathleven to Duncan II for knight service 1165 x 1172 William I grants Tough and Bogie to MacBeth (Aedh I?) witnessed by Duncan II 1172 David, Earl of Huntingdon, the King's brother, enacts charter at Markinch witnessed by Duncan II Earl of Fife 1173 X 1178 William I confirms the church of Markinch with lands and tithes also chapel of Kettle as gifts of Duncan II earl of Fife to St A's priory
1180 - 1190	
1200	1202 Agreement Between Bishop Roger and Duncan II re lands and patronage (Kilconqhhar, Kilmany, Cults etc) 1204 Earl Duncan II dies 1204 Earl Malcolm I succeeds 1204? Malcolm I confirms Cupar, Markinch, Scone, Kingskettle as grants made by his father 1204 x 1228 Malcolm gifts toft and one acre on northeast side of cemetery to church of Modhrust of Markinch
1210	1217 Malcolm I builds abbey at Culross
1220	1224 Dispute between Malcolm I and Prior of St A's over Pitenchagal (Pittenhaggles) resolved (coal and/or freestone?) 1228 Alexander II confirms Markinch church, tithes and lands as grant made by Duncan II 1229 Malcolm I dies without issue (nephew Malcolm II succeeds)
1230	
1240	1229 Malcolm I dies without issue (nephew Malcolm II succeeds) 1240 Bishop David grants churches of Markinch, Cupar and St Cyrus with all tithes and land to St A's Priory *"in propris usus"* 1243 Bishop David rededicates Markinch church to St John the Baptist and St Modhrust

up the disposable wealth and the network of contacts required for a major building project. This scenario would account for the involvement of Gillemichael's grandsons, Aed I and II, in William I's charter of around 1166.

However, an even earlier date cannot be ruled out given the proximity of the younger Constantine to the Scottish throne and likely access to good quality and innovative builders. We have only to look at buildings both secular and ecclesiastical in England and Normandy in the latter part of the 11th century and the early part of the 12th century to realise what could be achieved with the necessary resources, contacts and ambition.

The church at Markinch has never had a star role in the various histories of architecture in Scotland. Traditionally, the tower has been grouped together with Muthill, Dunning and Dunblane with little analysis of the church building attached to the tower, the context of its building or the identity of its builder. Occasionally it has been compared to St Rule's in St Andrews, and its fine stonework explained as a result of masons leaving one project and beginning another at a site nearby. Two of the attempts at dating St Rule's do not even make any mention of its local comparator at Markinch[34]. Gordon Donaldson puts both St Rule's and Markinch back as far as the 11th century on the basis of the two-light openings but recent writing ascribes the building to either the second quarter or the middle 12th century.[35] Most modern architectural guidebooks put its construction around 1200[36]. It is a remarkable variation for a building that has so much preserved in the form of its tower.

The evidence reviewed in this chapter does not point to the Bishop of St Andrews or the Prior as having much to do with the construction of the church. Instead it emphasises the fact that two out of the three donors to St Andrews Priory represented two parallel branches of the most powerful dynasty in Scotland outside the immediate royal family. Of note also is the fact that the building is in the heartland of their ancestral territory, close by their ancient place of legal assembly. The building has all the hallmarks of a church with a secular patronage.

---

[34] Fearnie, E. (1986) and Cameron, N. (1994)

[35] Fawcett, R. Scottish Medieval Churches (2002) Fawcett, R. *The Architecture of the Scottish Medieval Church* (2011)..

[36] Gifford, J. (1988). Pride, G. L. (1999) also accepted by Places of Worship in Scotland (SCHR)

In terms of the building's quality, the MacDuffs were closer to the Scottish Crown than any other element of the aristocracy. Any study of a church associated so closely with their name should put these facts at the centre of its enquiry. All the evidence points to the fact that the church was a MacDuff rather than an ecclesiastical initiative, the links to the Bishop of St Andrews being mainly historical and tied up with the gift of the church to Loch Leven Priory in the time of MacBeth. This should not cause us to overlook the influence of the Céli Dé community on the MacDuff family who had a close association with St Serf. The decoration on the tower and nave may be a clue to their influence on the design process and perhaps some of the other conservative elements in what is a technologically advanced building of considerable quality. The significance of the lozenge in early Christian iconography is set out by King[37] who summarises the main writings on the subject. It is a complex subject but perhaps deserves more attention given the prevalence of the symbol on early Scottish buildings.

Whether the patron of the building was a MacDuff earl or a MacDuff clan chief, we are dealing with the very highest echelons of Scottish society, both feudal and traditional. These are likely to be men that travelled with the Scottish royal family, led their armies, accompanied them on diplomatic missions and, on occasion, provided hostages as surety for peace. They would have had the opportunity to observe at first hand the most technically advanced building techniques and the most innovative designs anywhere in the British Isles. They would also have the resources to implement them rapidly within their own territories. A family one step away from the Scottish throne had a far reach when it came to securing both ideas and technical assistance. In addition, they were in the debt of Kings of Scotland who turned to them for support both military and in terms of feudal reform. Against this background we can cast a wide net when seeking the architectural influences and building expertise lying behind the apparently simple tower remaining as part of the church of at Markinch. This is picked up in the final chapter, but the church as a building has evolved and developed down through the centuries and the next section moves into the later medieval period.

---

[37] King, M. (2001) The Kilbroney Cross, the Book of Kells and an early Christian symbol of the Resurrection

Chapter 8

8. The Later Medieval Period

A building embellished or a building ignored?

As is the case with most Scottish towns, local history in Markinch has drawn heavily on the Statistical Accounts carried out by parish ministers in the late 18th and early 19th centuries. These took the spotlight away from the town's pre-Reformation history and in particular from social and political relationships at local level under the Catholic faith. They also downplayed the role of the prosperous local Roman Catholic landowning families which either disappeared or transformed their identity in the turbulent years of reform. Recent work has tried to redress the balance but it is still difficult to imagine the role of the old church in the community and indeed what it looked like as a building before it was comprehensively stripped and largely rebuilt most probably some time during the late 1600s. This chapter attempts to retrieve a few scraps from a period of the church's history that is in some ways even less well documented than the 12th century.

The 13th Century - decline of Markinch and its "Moustier"

In the early 13th century the earls of Fife consolidated their holdings throughout Scotland. Markinch was marginalised in favour of Falkland, acquired by marriage in the 1160s. Cupar became the regional seat of justice, an abbey was established by the Earl Malcolm I at Culross, and West Calder became an important family property[1]. Kilconquhar was a favoured family residence close to the ferry crossing giving access to MacDuff family landholdings in southern Scotland. The church at Markinch, despite having been gifted in the late 1160s, only came fully into the possession of the Priory of St Andrews towards the middle of the 13th century.

It was in the first quarter of the 13th century that Earl Malcolm I made a gift to Markinch Church of an acre of land once known as the Prior's land and

---

[1] Barrow, G. W. S. *The Earls of Fife in the 12th Century* Proceedings of the Society of Antiquaries 1953 p. 55 also by the same author *Robert Bruce*, pp 25, 331

now occupied by Mansefield. This piece of land was adjacent to a "toft" that had been gifted a generation earlier by his kinsman Aedh (II). This was known as the Vicar's land.[2] We know from a later charter that the first piece of property was known as the vicar's land and the second was known as the prior's land. In 1242, as noted in chapter 5, Bishop David de Bernham rededicated the church to St John the Baptist but Drostan remained as a joint dedication. Although the earls may have shifted their geographical focus elsewhere in the 13th century there is some evidence that the wider kinship group maintained a direct land ownership interest in the vicinity. Sibbald[3] refers to the existence in his time of a seal bearing the inscription *"MacDuffus de Balbirney"*. It would seem plausible that a senior member of the MacDuff family held Balbirnie, close by Markinch, at that time given that the land was the subject of a charter exchange between two branches of the MacDuff family in the mid 12th century. Markinch church was known locally as *"MacDuff's Kirk"* as late as the 19th century[4] but there appear to be no extant earlier records.

Towards the end of the thirteenth century in 1286, church possessions were further enlarged when William Valoniis, now in feudal possession of Dalginch granted the church a piece of land to the southeast of the acre previously referred to. The grant refers to the boundaries of what is now the Glebe, to the conferral of additional grazing rights belonging to the Brunton estate and to the gardener who presumably looked after the Prior's House. Also, for the first time it names the church vicar who lived just to the south of the prior's house where a new building now stands. His name was Ranulph[5]. With the patronage of the church now firmly in the hands of the Priory he is likely to have been their chosen appointee rather than a man selected by the MacDuff family, as was most probably the case a century earlier. The gift is made to the Church of St Andrew, in St Andrews on St Andrews Day reinforcing the shift in focus away from Markinch now that the Priory was in possession.

[2] St Andrews Liber, 420-421

[3] Sibbald 1710

[4] Parochial Directory for Fife and Kinross, Parish of Wemyss (Information probably from the Earl of Wemyss.) 1861, Russell, John R. 1882. The Kingdom - A Descriptive and Historical Handbook to Fife

[5] PNF Vol II

Within a few years, in 1298, King Edward I's army was pitched all around Markinch as he made his way from St Andrews to Dunfermline. His French speaking chronicler referred to the church as the "moustier" or minster, probably indicating not only its relative size and importance but also its dependency on the Priory at that time. Only three houses of any note were referred to as standing in Markinch indicating a decline in the town's fortunes, linked perhaps to a lessening of interest on the part of the earl. We have no record of any changes to the building during this period of history and no physical indications survive.

The 14th Century - a gift for a pope

During the next seventy years Scotland was riven with civil war, plague, famine and a struggle for national identity. The flickering light that history had been able to shed on Markinch Church during the 12th and 13th centuries almost goes out. We are left with a single reference from the Vatican Archives in 1332. This was the year when Bruce's infant son King David, after the briefest of periods on the throne, was deposed by Edward Balliol. Balliol was backed by the English King and by the exiled lords of Scotland who had been dispossessed by David's father. In September of 1332, after the battle of Halidon Hill, Balliol was crowned king. In November of that year, Thomas de Haddington the vicar of Markinch arrived in Avignon accompanied by two other clerics with a gift for Pope John XXII who had his palace located there. The gift was considerable, consisting of 1600 florins and a ruby ring (although 400 florins seem to have been withheld perhaps for travelling expenses)[6]. It was delivered on behalf of James, Bishop of St Andrews who fled Scotland after the coronation of David II, the predecessor of Edward Balliol. Bishop James Beane died in Flanders in 1330.[7] Was it a bribe, a payment for coronation anointing oil or a gift of gratitude for past support? No historical reference could be found to this event and the letter is quoted in full below.

The Vallances (also referred to as Valoniis or Valognes) seem to have re-granted some of their landholdings to the Moultrie family who became lords

[6]Calendar of entries in the Papal registers relating to Great Britain and Ireland. : Papal letters, Pub. 1893. Entry for 9 Kalends Nov 1332. "To John Leys, canon of Glasgow, Malcolm de Inverpeffri, canon of Dunblane and Thomas de Haddington, vicar of Markinch [....] acknowledging receipt of 1600 florins and a gold ring with a ruby bequeathed to the Pope by James, Bishop of St Andrews : the sum of 1600 florins and the ring having been sent by them, the executors, to the Pope during the lifetime of the said bishop."

[7] Maidment, J. *Analecta Scotica. Civil, Ecclesiastical and Literary History of Scotland 1837 (p. 6)*

of Markinch. Both family names appear as witnesses on a charter of 1384 and it is likely there were family burial aisles or small mausoleums for both within Markinch Church. Although their castle was at Seafield near Kinghorn, the Moultries were closely associated with Markinch until after the Reformation.

As regards the church building, once again virtually nothing is known. It may have been during this period of decline that the first roof rotted, hastened perhaps by the stripping of lead during the Wars of Independence but no records survive from this period. The new roofline shown etched against the east facing wall of the tower was lower and less steeply pitched than first. It also cut through the upper doorway arch indicating that the use of the building had changed. Perhaps religious or secular practices meant that an upper display area was no longer required or else the absence of the earl

Octagonal cresset (?) with interconnecting receptacles for oil

meant that an attic strongroom was not needed. The only artefact that may relate to this period is what seems to be a cresset used for burning tallow to provide light. It was found in the garden of Mansefield.

The next Markinch vicar to surface in the Vatican archives is Henry de Lichton (or Leighton) who began his illustrious career around 1392. He went on to become bishop of both Moray and Aberdeen. He was responsible for much of the building of Aberdeen cathedral, dedicated to St Machar and he served James I as ambassador to England, France and Italy. His tenure of Markinch seems to have been brief, perhaps indicating that Markinch was seen at that time as an easy posting close to St Andrews or perhaps a first step on the ecclesiastical ladder.

The 15th Century - church careers and financial rewards

No written 15th references to the church building could be found and we can only trace its history through occasional references to its vicars in the Vatican archives. Existing histories of Markinch ignore this source and recent research within the framework of this project has aimed to fill in pre-Reformation gaps in the church's history. In 1423 the career churchman John Elwalde, rector of Kirkandrews in Kirkcudbright, appears in Rome to seek further advancement. He seems to have had revenue from Markinch as a supplementary income along with Selkirk Regis in Teviotdale.[8] Elwalde demonstrates that by the 15th century an absentee cleric could pick up 'prebends' around the country with little thought for the needs of the parishioners.

John Feldew was another Markinch vicar seen from the archives in 1432 to hold several benefices including Linlithgow and St. Nicholas, the leper hospital to the south of St Andrews. He was succeeded in turn by John Winchester, a son of wealthy parents and also a canon of Aberdeen Cathedral. At that time, the annual vicar's income from Markinch was £17 with an additional £7 from the hospital in St Andrews.

Later in 1481 we find a reference to Robert Lennox, vicar of Markinch and by 1486 a papal letter sets out a proposed arrangement between Walter Monypenny, prior of St Serfs on Loch Leven and John Hepburn prior of St Andrews Priory.[9] Under the agreement Monypenny gives up St Serfs to Hepburn in exchange for the 'tithes of sheaves lawfully belonging to the Priory of St Andrews in the parishes of Markinch and Pitulloch (Petinolloch)'. Great detail is entered into as to who should get what according to different market conditions. If times were hard, Monypenny was guaranteed a basic income from the hard-pressed peasants. If times were good he had to hand over the surplus to the St Andrews Priory. It is just a glimpse into the machinations and politicking of the time as career churchmen increasingly

---

[8] Calendar of entries in the Papal registers relating to Great Britain and Ireland. : Papal letters Pub.. 1893

[9] ditto

blurred the secular and the ecclesiastical aspects of their positions. Another vicar, Robert Levanay surfaces in 1495[10], just before the turn of the century.

By now the name MacDuff had disappeared from the locality to be replaced perhaps by their descendants, the families of Wemyss, Balbirnie and possibly Schethum (Shythrum), now named after their land rather than their kin group. A member of the Wemyss family, "Andrew Vemys" was the curate of Markinch and several of his chaplains were witnesses to a land transaction whereby Andrew Schethum, a small landowner on a holding straddling the River Leven, transferred his property to the Lundie family. Around 1500 we have a reference to a Thomas Diksone[11], vicar of Markinch involved in a dispute about coal deposits.

The 16th Century - an energetic prior and a murdered cardinal

It is clear from the faint outline of a crozier that it is Prior John Hepburn's shield that is set into the eastern wall of Markinch church although it might be noted that his brother James was Bishop of St Andrews at the time. John was an energetic builder, responsible for constructing the town walls of St Andrews and co-founder of St Leonard's College in St Andrews. As Prior at St Andrews, Hepburn was rector of Markinch Parish Church. His plaque and its

[10] Special Collections Dept., University of St Andrews. Non-collegiate papers of the University relating to privileges and titles UYUY100-119

[11] Charters of the Hospital of Soltre, of Trinity College Edinburgh etc. Vicar of Markinch vs Lord Balgonie. Bannatyne Club 1859

significance to the dating of the chancel has been discussed in a previous chapter.

It is difficult to be certain but he seems to have been responsible for some renovation work, perhaps the insertion of a window into the chancel. The lower, less steeply sloping roof line etched out by the raggle marks on the tower may relate to his period of renovation. Perhaps he was also responsible for re-roofing and shorter rafters appear to have been cut through the stone upper doorway arch. During the early 16th century, longer timbers could not be procured due to lack of suitable timber (the ship Great Michael was built in 1505 and is reputed to have stripped Fife bare of timber). Whatever else Hepburn may have done to the building it has been effaced by later rebuilding work.

A carved stone dragon supporting a triangular shelf found in a neighbouring garden in Commercial Street seems to date from the first half of the 16th century. A piscina (or washing basin) with a very similar carving is to be seen in Seton Collegiate Chapel East Lothian and the Setons of Balbirnie held land locally during the 16th century.[12] The Markinch object may have been where the sacrament was placed during the mass. It is of course possible that Hepburn's changes to the existing church fabric were considerable. If so, then almost all of the evidence disappeared in the subsequent post-Reformation reconstructions, to be recycled or dumped, probably in the north eastern corner of the churchyard.

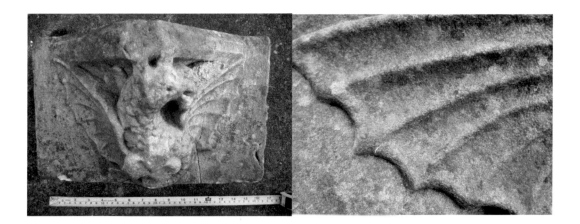

---

[12] Fawcett, R. Scottish Medieval Churches. p. 276

During the 16th century there would most likely have been smaller altars and family burial sites at different points around the walls. Descriptions survive of an area set aside for the Beatons (Bethunes) of Balfour with two full-length marble effigies of David Beaton and Elizabeth Monypenny his wife, parents of Cardinal David Beaton assassinated in 1546[13]. As wealthy heritors the Bethunes would have been generous benefactors and it might be wondered whether the carved wooden panels that once adorned nearby Balfour House were removed from Markinch. The Wardlaw family stopped burying their dead in the 1620s leaving both their "aisle" inside the kirk and their burial lair outside to the Bethunes[14] to whom they were related by marriage.

Beaton had earlier employed the royal master craftsman Mansioun to carve a brass plaque for his mother in 1541. As the son of a local heritor, the young David Beaton no doubt celebrated mass in Markinch Church and probably returned as a student to witness its renovation by builders paid by Prior Hepburn. Beaton's death was a matter of national and international importance impacting on the future of both church and state. His assassins were local men from Leslie and Kirkcaldy involved in longstanding family feuds. Beaton's body, wrapped in lead and stuffed into a barrel lay for weeks on the foreshore of St Andrews before it was removed to a secret location. Local tradition maintains that the body was eventually buried in the family vault at Markinch but Sanderson leaves open the issue of his place of burial[15].

The kind of dubious church benefices that we have glimpsed at Markinch during the 15th and early 16th century sowed seeds of resentment and reforming ideas amongst ordinary people right across Scotland. This led to the old church's downfall and a radical Reformation with Fife at the epicentre. In Markinch we have little evidence of how the reformed kirk looked inside but we can imagine a wholesale rearrangement of the interior designed to wipe away all traces of the old order refocusing the congregation away from the altar at the east end and towards the pulpit, usually centrally placed on the southern wall. This may have taken place in stages as the church see-sawed between Presbyterian and Episcopalian ministers more or less linked to the major heritors.

[13] Herkless, J. & Hannay, R.K. 1913 The Archbishops of St Andrews

[14] St Andrews University Special Collection Dept. ms -37860

[15] Sanderson, M. H. B. (2001). Cardinal of Scotland. John Donald Publishers

It may even be the case that Pictish and popish ornamentation were bracketed together by the Protestant iconoclasts, as the standing stone known as the Stob Cross seems to have been heavily defaced on both sides around this period in an attempt perhaps to simplify its outline and appearance. It may have been that in this process of destruction the tower was saved partly because of its utility and partly due to its austere appearance and lack of ornamentation. There is, however, evidence that the decorated frieze around the tower arch was removed with a chisel.

The exterior of the tower in the later 16th century would probably have looked very similar to the way it looked when completed in the 12th century. The spire and the roof, constructed from perishable timber, would no doubt have suffered from the ravages of war and decay. Perhaps the low pyramidical roof shown on the drawings of 1805 dates from this period. The great western arch between tower and nave, and probably the chancel arch would still have been visible, from inside the place of worship although the altar screen and other religious trappings would have given way to a bare public room that was rearranged for the living, not the dead. Tombs and effigies within the church were disposed of. It is possible that many bodies were exhumed from under the floor and deposited along with unwanted church trappings to the east and north east of the church where a retaining wall was built. As an inscription in nearby Collessie churchyard put it :-

Defyle not Christ's Kirk with your carion

a solomn sait for God's service prepared

for praier, preaching and communion

your byrial should be in the kirkyaird.

This admonition most likely applied to Markinch as well. During the survey some limited exploration was carried out under the floorboards but the ground appeared to be free of burials. Local tradition speaks of thousands of burials that were cleared out from under the church. This is likely to be a gross exaggeration but there are signs that the congregation firstly tried to cover over the floor with stone flags but later resorted to a mass clear-out when boards were laid in the late 19th century. The radar survey only picked out one possible large pre-Reformation burial and that was at a spot corresponding to the centre of the chancel arch.

Building Archaeology - all traces gone?

Very little investigation has been carried out on the church as it existed between the 12th and the 19th centuries. The work on the tower demonstrated that there might have been dado panelling at two different periods in the building's history. Signs of later timber furnishings are shown by baton marks and wooden pegs for fixing dado panelling that would once have lined the walls from the doorway through the arch and into the church. There are two separate sets of pegs, small round ones and larger square ones indicating panelling at two separate dates, one before and one after the insertion of the door in the late 18th century. Horizontal grooves for batons have also been cut into the stone. A coating of red stain or paint has been applied after the panels have been removed as the pegs and grooves are painted over. Finally, plaster has been applied over the paint, probably later in the 19th century with a skim of cement following in the 20th century.

Conclusion

The lack of written references to Markinch church during the three hundred years prior to the Reformation would indicate that it rapidly declined from a major place of worship close by the earl's place of legal assembly to a quiet parish church largely dependent upon the Priory of St Andrews. Tithes would have been drawn away gradually but the Priory's right of preferment meant that the MacDuffs probably lost interest in the building, particularly as they shifted their focus to other parts of Scotland during the 13th century. Local kinsmen, most notably the Wemyss, Balfours and Balbirnie families probably maintained links to the building due to ancestral burials.   In the 19th century the Wemyss family were allocated loft space immediately above the former chancel and the Balfour family grave seems to have been transferred to a plot on the outside of the church just north of the chancel when the building was enlarged in the early 19th century.

Although a close examination of the later medieval period has revealed little about the building itself, it has enabled us for the first time to record the names of the vicars who were overlooked by post-Reformation historians. We do not know why Prior Hepburn took a special interest in Markinch church but it may have been in a ruinous condition by the 16th century. His repairs were probably minor but, as with all his other building and repair projects in St Andrews including the Cathedral and St Rules, he seems to have left his mark by embedding in the walls a shield embellished with his coat of arms. There is no evidence that he widened the building or added a southern aisle along the lines of Muthil. He was probably content to proclaim to any visitor that he had spent money on the building, no doubt as he would see it to the glory of God rather than in pursuit of any career advancement. He was elected archbishop but despite all his good works this was not accepted by the Pope.

Chapter 9

9. Pushing out the Walls
The progressive disappearance of the old church

This chapter focusses upon the gradual disappearance and transformation of the 12th century building. As noted previously, it is apparent from raggle lines (roof marks) on the tower, visible from inside the present day loft space, that major re-roofing and widening projects were undertaken, first a renewal of the roof (date unknown), then an expansion to the south (17th century), then an expansion the north associated with a heightening of the roof (early 19th century) and finally a project that pierced new ground floor windows and added stairs flanking the vestibule at the back (late 19th century). The following is an attempt to set out what we know about the building campaigns using primary written sources as well as building detail and stylistic comparisons. This is very much work in progress and church documents are still being transcribed.

Re-roofing - Date Unknown

At some point prior to the Reformation the roof was completely renewed but with the use of shorter trusses than had been the case for the 12th century building. This may indicate lack of resources or simply lack of trees of the required length within reasonable hauling distance. The roof sat on the same 12th century walls but its lower profile cut through the finely carved voussoirs of the arch above the little door linking the tower with the roof space of the nave. It may have been necessary to replace the original roof because of damage caused by the removal of lead during the wars of independence or it could have been part of Prior Hepburn's renovations in the early 16th century. No other vestiges of this rebuilding campaign survive except perhaps the traces of a small chancel window above Hepburn's shield on the east wall. It might be noted that, judging from the raggle marks, St Rule's in St Andrews had its roof changed on two occasions but it is not clear whether one of these may in fact have been a heightening as a result of Bishop Robert's improvements.

Widening to the South - 17th Century

The raggle marks also show that at some point the heritors enlarged the church by demolishing the south walls of the old nave and chancel and replacing them with a rubble-built wall incorporating many of the fine 12th century ashlar stone blocks. This most probably occurred after the Reformation and well into the 17th century. It produced an architecturally coherent south facing facade eliminating the distinction between nave and chancel. The illustrated cross section shows that the newly built south wall was the same height as the original back wall that was presumably left in place until the 19th century. The roof-line protruded slightly above the line of the present day roof and a section of string course had to be removed to accommodate it. The 12th century remains are shown in red and the post - Reformation extension in blue, including the Leslie tomb. There may have later been a form of loft constructed between the tomb and the church as a kind of extension but no physcal evidence remains due to later 19th century work.

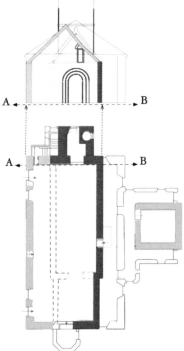

Markinch Parish Church
Post-Reformation extension to the south

Recent research[1] has begun into records from the 17th century. In 1637 a new bell was fitted and in the same year a contract was issued with a Kirkcaldy glazier for the upkeep of the windows. A reference to a single "loft" or gallery is made in 1638. There is an entry for 1653 relating to the purchase of seven and a half ells of "wyre" or window glazing bars indicating substantial work of either renewal or renovation at that time.

[1] Carried out by Maureen Brand and Pete Wadley 2013

Carpenters and slaters were employed and much lime used from 1683 to 1690. The work relates mainly to the flooring of the building, roof work and the construction of wooden lofts. Particularly significant is the purchase of "trees and deals for the kirk" in 1685 (£18/6s/7p), similar materials for a loft in 1687 (probably a second loft) costing £13 and the cost of a slater for "pointing the steeple", also in 1687.

The Reverend William Stevenson who scanned the session records in 1882 came across no firm evidence to date the first rebuilding. There seems to be no reference to the hiring of stone masons to carve quoin stones, windows or doors during this period and we can not yet be certain when the actual extension to the south took place although some time during the late 1680s would be a reasonable guess based upon the available evidence. The burgh was granted burgh of barony status in 1672 by Charles II but more significantly perhaps, David Leslie the 3rd Earl of Leven, secured several lucrative government positions in the late 1680s following his support for William of Orange a few years earlier. It may be that building contracts passed directly though the hands of this powerful heritor rather than through the Kirk Session. It is an area for future research.

Without an unambiguous written record we have only the evidence of the stones themselves. Other than the quoins and the surrounds of windows and doors, the quality of the stonework on the south wall was clearly not important to the builders, and it is believed the walls would have been harled or rendered. The rubble of the old Norman style church can still be seen incorporated into the south wall including three chip-cut decorated blocks, and many ashlar blocks from the old building were reused. They tend to be regularly cut and with a veined appearance matching those on the tower. The outline of a segmental arch in pinkish stone can still be seen on the southern wall and this may well have been the main entrance when the building was first enlarged, probably replacing a more elaborate 12th century door. Although the red coloured stone used around the crown of the arch makes it stand out from the rest of the wall it is likely to have been an original part of that wall.

Other stones on the wall, for example from around the windows, have both pink and greyish-white tints, and it is clear that both shades were present in the same quarry. Lower down on both the arch and on the doorway at the eastern end, 12th century yellowish veined ashlar seems to have been recut to form the jambs or uprights. The narrower two of the four long windows on the south wall may date from the time of the wall construction, at least in their lower sections but the sketch below seems to suggest that they were originally narrower. Further dating evidence for the southern expansion may yet be gathered from the way iron cleats have been used to fix this building's roof to the tower. The triple keystone arches above the south facing windows do not help us with dating as the arches were evidently replaced in the early 19th century when the wall was heightened. The photograph show the section of broached stonework that was added at this time.

No precise date has been arrived at for the building of the Leslie Aisle, the former mausoleum that now serves as the church's entrance vestibule. It has been enveloped by the flanking staircases installed in 1884 and considerably altered by the installation of a wide door at the same time. It still has fine groin vaulting and a series of burial inscriptions that seem to relate to the Leslies although no firm attribution has been agreed. If the AL refers to either the first or the second Alexander Leslie, Lord Leven then their recorded deaths would date the mausoleum to the mid 17th century although it might be slightly earlier. Arrow sharpening marks can be seen near the door which was pierced in the north wall during the 19th century. These may suggest an early foundation course that has been built upon unless the stone is recycled. The building was once separate from the church but may later have had a a family loft installed. It once had narrow slit windows on the ground floor that were, according to plans, blocked up in the 19th century. A door and a stairway once led to a burial chamber below.

The Balfour entrance was most probably added in the late 17th century. This construction has been analysed by architect James Jack who shows that it was added to several times during its history. It probably dates from the time when the southerly extension was built and may once have been an open set of steps, perhaps with a wooden balustrade. First the landing and then the steps to the landing seem to have been enclosed. Windows were inserted to provide light for the Balfour family who used the entrance regularly until recent times. The plaster work at the top of the stairs is likely to conceal the masonry join between the 12th century and the post-Reformation building.

18th century changes

There is only one existing rough sketch of the church as it may have

appeared during the 18th century and that is on the Taylor map[2] of Markinch. This appears to have been drawn originally in the 18th century and subsequently added to several times over the subsequent century. It is not clear whether the first of the two dates is 1704 or 1764 but the appearance of the church may not have changed much during that time period. It shows the post-Reformation south wall with the arched doorway, apparently in use. Two other smaller doors can also be

[2] The original is believed to be in St Andrews University Special Collections Dept but only a photocopy produced for research in the 1980s can be located (see Ken Wilkie)

seen, one in the middle of the wall and the other at the west end. The sketch also shows a piended or hipped roof and a close inspection of the church today will show the old eaves line running around the south wall and and along the east wall which had been raised a few feet above the old chancel gable.

It is unlikely that the church was added to the map at a date later than 1765 as the original map appears to be drawn around the sketch of the building using different scales. The church windows on the sketch appear narrow but it may not be an accurate representation in all respects. Only two lower windows are evident (not quite aligned with those above) and we know from the 1788 heritors' minutes that two further small windows were added when the two end doors were blocked. We can conclude that he sketch is likely to be a representation of the extended front wall, probably close to its original post-Reformation rebuilt state. It therefore follows that the wall was most likely built prior to 1765 and possibly before 1704 if that is the first date. This is further evidence contradicting the 1786 date found in the guidebooks. There are gaps in the early 18th century church records (1708-12 and 1715-88) but a date for the church extension is more likely to be late 17th century than 18th based on the references to work carried out in the Session Records that do exist.

Heritors' records do not begin until 1788 and the first recorded meeting agreed to

"shut up the east and west doors in the front of the church and to place a window of four feet square in each door and to open two new doors in the east and the west of the church as nearly in the centre of the communion tables as the situation will admit".

New windows and shutters were to be manufactured as well as a new pulpit and a reader's desk. The function of these new square windows would have been to allow light into the dark recesses under the galleries or lofts that individual heritors and townsfolk had haphazardly constructed over the years. It is likely that the re-cut door into the tower was one of the two new doors sanctioned at this meeting as well as the entrance through what is now the boiler house. The triple-keystone arch above the tower's door is similar to windows inserted into several Scottish churches around this time[3] but more comparative research is required on this topic. As noted in the previous section, matching keystones may have been later added to the top of the long front windows when the church was heightened early in the 19th century. This may have given the south wall an 18th century appearance contributing to the perception that the wall was built in the 1780s.

The heritors further agreed in 1788 that; -

"*...the whole church shall be seated on one uniform plan [.....] at the expense of the whole heritors [.....] proportioned to their several valued rents.*"

The west, north and east galleries were divided up in an elaborate way according to the heritors' rental with special attention being given to the best viewing areas at the front of the galleries. The allocation included a number of communion tables which must have been a feature of the old kirk. The assembled heritors agreed "amicably" to furnish the sum of £270 towards the work which also included re-plastering and roof repairs.

Hunter (1984) believed that the church was re-built in 1786 around the same time as the manse which was refurbished by Thomas Barclay, a master mason from Balbirnie. This is repeated in Gifford's book on the Buildings of Fife (1988). However, neither the heritors' minutes nor the Statistical Account written in the 1790s make any reference to such a major rebuilding. If this refers to the building of the south wall then it is unlikely that windows would be inserted into a wall which had only recently been completed. If it refers to the extension to the north then it is clear that this took place some years later, in the early 19th century, as we shall examine in the next section.

As the 1788 heritors' minutes show, two of the lower square windows on the south wall were added just prior to 1788. The insertion of one of these windows would have been accompanied by the blocking up of the arched entrance at the western end of the south wall. The now blocked entrance and many of the quoin stones used to block it are likely to have been recycled from the original 12th century building, perhaps, judging by their size, they came from the part of the west wall of the tower now occupied by the doorway. This may reinforce the view that there was no 12th century door in this wall or that it was very small.

---

[3] e.g. St Mungo's Church Penicuik (1746), Aberdour Parish Church (1790), St Andrews, Dundee (1770s)

The Early 19th Century - Extension to the North

The heritors met in December 1805 to hear a report that the roof needed replacing. Reconvening in February the following year, they resolved that it would be cost effective to enlarge the entire church. The minutes state that :-

" the church of Markinch was quite insufficient to contain the population of the parish. They therefore unanimously agreed to enlarge the church so as to contain at least four hundred people more - the enlargement to be at the back of the church."

The meeting agreed to write to Alexander Leslie of Largo and James Barclay of Edinburgh for detailed plans and specifications. The following month (7th March 1806) the heritors agreed that James Barclay's plan was superior. Another plan exists in an inferior hand showing a curved pew arrangement and no separate entrance for the Balfour family. This may be the rejected plan.

The drawing showing proposed work at the back of the church no longer exists but the front elevation and the upstairs and downstairs plans remain in the Leslie-Melville (Earl of Leven) archives. Fortunately good drawings of 1884 show in faint red dotted lines the outline of what was actually built, most likely during the major 1805 alterations.

The front elevation drawing of 1805 shows that the intention was to heighten the wall and the roof (a few feet higher than actually built) but

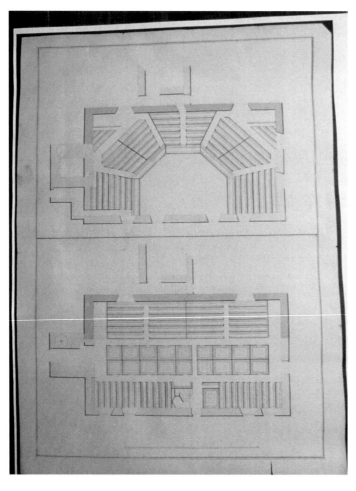

otherwise no major changes were envisaged to the front of the building as it then stood.

The earl, having examined the plans, said in a letter to the minister dated 1806 -

"The elevation is I believe the same as it now is and with a sloping new blue roof, nothing can look more frightful but by a few trifling alterations if agreeable to the Heritors it might be corrected.

1st by making a corresponding door which may be very useful as I observe but 2 doors for the use of 1000 persons

2nd by making a painted oval or circular window over the door between the two windows

3rd By making a cornish (sic) or freize under the sklates (sic) of a proper dimension so as to give a full effect

And last - let me add- how much will the whole edifice be improved by raising a spire on the tower or crowning it with pinnacles at the four corners. Indeed it has long struck me as one of the most horrid and disgraceful specimens of art, that ever was sanctioned by the gentlemen of taste composing the Heritors of the Parish."

It is clear that this letter refers to the above elevation associated with the plan below, and so the drawing and its plans can be safely dated to 1805. This places the northerly extension into the early 19th century rather than the late

18th as had previously been assumed. It also clearly distinguishes the early 19th century northerly extension from the much earlier southerly extension, the two being frequently conflated.

The "corresponding door" referred to in the letter is not shown on the drawing but is surely the small south east door that must have been inserted in place of the square window shown on the elevation. The circular window and the cornice referred to were also most likely added to the project on the advice of Lord Leven.

The minute of 28th March 1806 agreed to most of Lord Leven's requests including lathing and plastering, provision of cornices inside and out, wooden flooring under the pews and stone paving of the passages. They did not agree at this meeting to his proposals to replace the spire, preferring to carry out repairs to the existing structure. James Barclay was to be requested to furnish a fresh copy of the plans as the earl had not returned his version. The spire, not shown on the drawings, was not completed until 1807.

No elevation has yet been found showing the proposed elevations of the north facing wall of the church at this time and these may have ended up in the hands of the builders. The broad outline can, however, be extrapolated from the surviving plans of 1884. They show what is presumably the existing fabric of the building shaded in pink with proposed building works, including two large windows, shaded in grey. If this interpretation is correct then this provides further confirmation that the extension to the north took place around this time (c1806), not 1786 as had previously been thought[4]. The 1805 plans also show proposals for two internal staircases to the east and the west of the main chamber giving access to the balcony. The Leslie-Melville balcony in the middle is shown as accessed by means of a separate stair between the existing family crypt and the proposed new part of the church. Separate entrance for the Balfour family is also shown. All the internal bench seating and box pews are shaded grey, indicating that the refurbishments involved replacing the timber work on a considerable scale. Planking from this earlier balcony was found during work under the floorboards of the western part of the balcony in 2015.

Also worth noting on these plans is the fact that stair access to what became the Balfour section of the gallery is shown in pink as "existing". Three

---

[4] Hunter (1983), Gifford (1988)

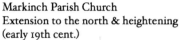

Markinch Parish Church
Extension to the north & heightening
(early 19th cent.)

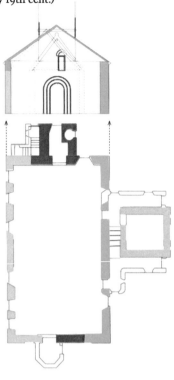

doors to the main place of worship are shown - in the west through the tower, in the south through what became the 19th century vestry and in the east through the apse that is now the boiler house. The west door through the tower is clearly shown on the plan as existing, not proposed. This reinforces the view that the tower door dates from the 1788 improvements. However, the new balcony required a support beam that pieced the voussoirs of the arch and so a wooden lintel seems to have been inserted lower down the arch as part of a new doorway. All of these entrances are now blocked being replaced with the north porch and the existing main entrance through the former family vault.

The tooling on the upper stone work of the south wall confirms that this wall was heightened at the same time as the church was widened to the north. As noted above this would have meant heightening the existing windows as well as inserting the round window referred to in Leslie-Melville's letter. The 1805 elevations show the old window layout rather than what was eventually built and it is worth noting that there is no depiction of decorative keystones. It is likely, however, that the triple keystone arches were inserted at this time as a later addition along with the round window and the cornices following Leslie-Melvilles intervention. Perhaps the keystone motif was modelled on the existing west door inserted seventeen years earlier thus complicating the dating of the south wall.

When the estimates came in, it was Thomas Barclay of Presty Hall near Balbirnie Bridge that secured the mason's contract by a mere 9 pence at £134/19/3 provided he sign alongside James Barclay and George Barclay. Presumably these were relatives but men whose work was already known to the heritors. Roof work and plastering added a further £167/15/6 and woodwork to be provided by Alexander Leslie of Largo came in at £807/10/9 making a grand total of £1,110/5/6. The subsequent transfer of the windows and some unforeseen plaster work added to the cost but he seems from later accounts to have delivered the work inside the budget estimate. Final approval of works was carried out on behalf of the heritors by Robert Balfour, a St Andrews architect.

Heritors' minutes of 1806 show that there was a later agreement to take old windows from the front of the building and reinsert them at the back as part of the overall widening project. This accords with the mullion style, glass and the dimensions of the windows, front and back, as they exist today. Although the timber frame and the glass seem to have been transferred, the surrounding stone and the triple keystone window arches at the back of the church have been apparently cut specially to hold the frames. Only the two longer, central windows were repositioned in this way and the surrounding stonework at the front has been reused to hold the newly inserted wider frames. The two smaller arched windows on either side were simply heightened, and their former height can be observed from the joins in the carefully matched stones surrounding the wooden frames. There is a reference in the 1807 minutes to Alexander Leslie, the wright (joiner) adding "front windows enlarging -£12" to his overall estimate for the carpentry work. This presumably refers to the construction of the frames and the insertion of glass as the related stonework would have been carried out by the mason.

It is not clear whether the tower's spire on the drawings was a proposal or a representation of what already existed but Lord Leven's comment that it should be replaced in his letter of 1806 eventually had an impact upon the heritors. Although the original proposals involved simply repairing the existing steeple, it was decided in 1807 that a new one should be built and it was completed that summer. The proposal was not to touch the "arch" at the top of the building but to demolish the pyramid roof above it and replace it with a stone structure. The "arch" presumably refers to the stone dome that now underpins the steeple but there may have been a timber predecessor.

Timber and stone repairs to the interior of the tower appear from the minutes to have been carried out at the same time. The replacement spire cost £209 and was designed by James Barclay with Thomas Barclay as the mason. It is remarkably similar to the top of St Andrew's Church spire in Dundee designed by James Craig and he may well have provided the inspiration. It was octagonal and designed to offer as little wind resistance as possible. Early drawings show that when first built, it was an architecturally well-balanced structure with four pinnacles at each corner in picturesque late medieval rather than Norman style. The removal of the pinnacles later in the century did not enhance the structure but probably went some way to placating public opinion which seemed to have been in favour of removing the spire altogether.

All the seats outlined in the plan of 1805 were, on the building's completion, carefully divided up according to the value of the land possessed by the heritors who co-financed the building operation. The elaborate system of preferential selection employed in 1788 was replaced by a simpler system. Land ownership and acreage was compared to what it had been the last time there was a major call on the heritors' financial contribution which seems to have been as early as 1637. The seats were then allocated by the inch to each of the land holdings in the parish, all of which seem to have contributed to the cost. Such an estate-based solution to the allocation of seats created a grievance with the small merchants and landholders of the burgh. In 1808, their appointed spokesperson Thomas Thomson pointed out to the heritors that in the 1740s they had sanctioned the building of a gallery by the "feuers" at their own expense but that these ancient rights had been lost in the 1790s when their loft was extended by the Wemyss family.

In the early years of the 19th century the senior heritor was Lord Leven, representing the Leslie-Melville family and, as has been noted, the committee agreed several concessions for him ensuring that the family vault was protected during the building operations and that his tenants were well served in the allocation of seats. When they sold out to a branch of the Balfour family around 1824, the scene was set for further changes as another influential family rose to the pre-eminent position.

A feature of Markinch church is the curious 5-sided apse-like porch appended to the east gable. This now serves as a boiler house but has proved difficult to date. The doorway of the porch once faced south but was transferred to the north wall when the boiler was put in towards the end of the 19th century. A window facing east has also been blocked. A double width doorway appears on the drawings of 1805 but the porch does not and so it most likely dates from slightly later in the 19th century. The door's position on the gable end would have been at the mid point of the 18th century gable. It would have been off-centre from the original chancel and so is unlikely to date from either the 12th century or be part of any early 16th century work by Hepburn. The entrance has a curious flattened arch, a possible parallel being on the north wall of a simple 18th century farm building less than a mile away at Brunton Barns. The low floor level within the porch may well have been the level of the rest of the church prior to the 1884 raising of the floor level.

Old photographs from the middle of the century show that there was a vestry built around the middle door on the south wall. It was probably built in the early 1800s but is not shown on the drawing of 1805 (although the minister's door is shown). It was demolished towards the end of the same century. The raggle lines formed by the roof of this vestry can still be seen on the front of the building and the foundations were picked up in the resistivity work carried out during 2013. Recent research into the heritors' minutes found that in 1884 senior heritor Mr Balfour gave immediate consent to its demolition with the comment that .... *it is a hideous creation which quite spoils the south side of the church*[5].

The Late 19th Century

In 1884 plans were drawn up by James Gillespie (Scott, the other member of the famous partnership joined the firm a year later). Further significant changes to the layout of the main place of worship were planned. This time the proposed alterations were coloured brown. The changes all seem to have been implemented over the coming years and broadly speaking produced the building that we know today. Changes include a blocking of the east and west doors (i.e. through the arch to the tower) as well as the little door in the south wall used by the minister. This time the public entrance was to be straight through the tomb of the Leslie-Melvilles, something that would have been tantamount to sacrilege in the early part of the century, but by the 1880s the

[5] Identified by Maureen Brand Jan 2016

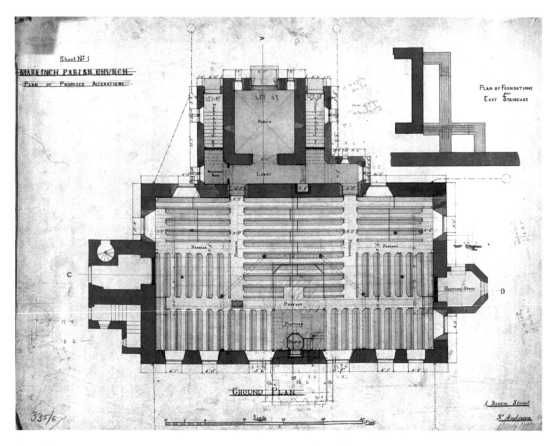

family was no more represented in the parish. The entrance vestibule that we see today was created by widening both doors of the tomb, blocking the ancient slit windows on either side and

inserting new ones facing north. The great "monumental panel" of the Leslie-Melville family was taken off south wall of the tomb and relocated within the church.

Probably for the first time in their history, the tower and the kirk were separated by a solid wall blocking the arch. The 1884 plans were so detailed that a ghost image of the earlier layout and seating plan in red hatching can be seen. This enables us to confirm that the 1805 seating layout and access plans were actually carried into effect.

The south facing elevation shows that little here was to be changed in 1884 except, as noted, for the minister's door being blocked associated with the demolition of the vestry. Another enigmatic pencil sketch of an arch is just visible on the right hand side of the drawing but it is not clear whether this is

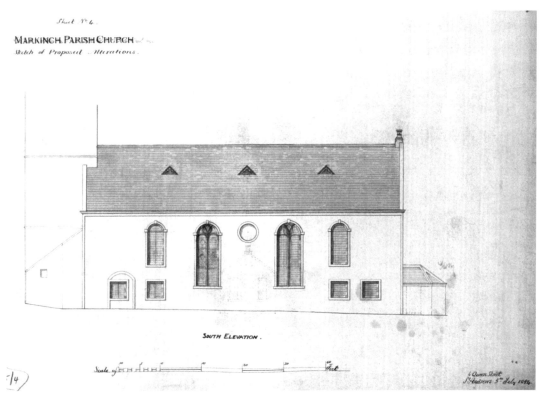

a representation of the chancel arch based upon remains found at the time. The ventilation ducts also seem to be a proposal on this drawing.

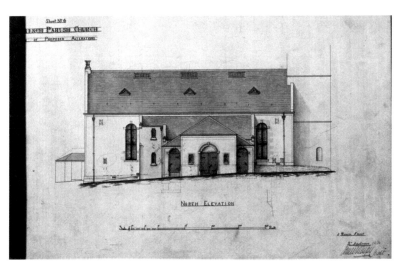

Most radical of all, however, on the north elevation, the plans envisaged flanking both sides of the mausoleum with external staircases replacing the internal ones that took up so much space in the previous layout. This innovative arrangement also created a downstairs and an upstairs lobby and a minister's room in the space between the former family tomb and the main body of the kirk where the Leslie-Melville access stairs had once been wedged. In order to make room for the western staircase, a complete window at the back of the church was transposed several feet towards the tower. Additional windows, all newly glazed, were inserted at ground level on the east wall and on the west wall next to the tower.

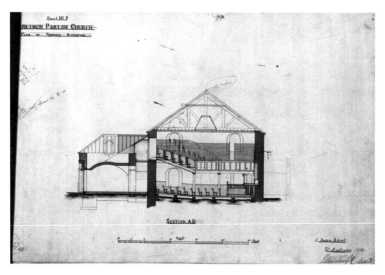

A cross section shows that most of the timber seating, joists and flooring was replaced at this time although the gallery facing is unshaded, indicating that it remained from the previous refurbishments in 1805. The box pews were to be removed and a close examination today of the panels against the walls indicates that they may well be the recycled remains of these early 18th century features. The roof of the old mausoleum, or vestibule as it was to become, was tied in to the main building across the newly created corridor.

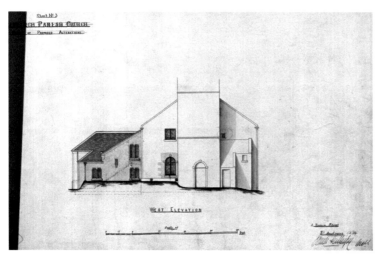

The west elevation shows one of the flanking stairs from the side as well as the window proposed at this time. The window must have cut into the quoin stones of the old nave. This would have made it impossible to identify the join had earth not been moved from around the tower revealing the lower courses of the 12th century building. It will be noted that no works were proposed for the tower at that time.

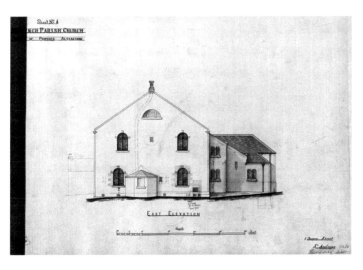

The east elevation shows clearly the two ground level gable end windows that were proposed for this refurbishment as well as the flanking stairs. It seems from old photographs that they were not inserted until some years later, again destroying some of the evidence of the 12th century corner stones. The outline of the old vestry is also visible in hatched outline as well as the chimney cut into the wall above the boiler.

Other changes that we know about from heritors' minutes include improved heating and ventilation, pointing, re-slating, the installation of

roans and the replacement of the ceiling and rafters, although the cornice was retained. The total estimate was around £1000 but we have not yet located the final invoice. The key selling point in the architect's report was "comfort and convenience" and he played upon the fact that the building was outmoded and below the standard of most modern places of worship[6].

The plans from 1884 do not depict the spire but there must have been a significant change at around this time. An 1864 sketch shows the pinnacles, the parapet and the minister's vestry that was once attached to the front of the building. The lower windows on the east wall have yet to be inserted but a small door (now blocked) near the north east corner door is illustrated as well as a north facing door on the porch. The oldest photographs that we have also show a crenellated parapet with four stone pinnacles, one at each corner. In the photos taken in the early years of the 20th century both the pinnacles and the battlements are gone. The shield that is played for at the annual Markinch Highland Games also has the pinnacled spire etched in silver, perhaps copied (with some inaccuracies such as the round window) from an older photograph.

The 20th Century

The next set of surviving plans were drawn up on the eve of the First World War. The project involved heightening the roof with ornamental woodwork, carved bosses and gothic style corbels of a totally different design to the elegant Georgian lines that had characterised the building's interior for over a hundred years. After the War, for whatever reason, the plans for the roof heightening were laid aside. Around the same time it was agreed to install an organ and a new heating system. This project went ahead entailing the extension of a trench originally laid for the installation of pipes in the 1880s. The gas driven bellows for the organ were installed in the tower and the new boiler in the porch abutting the east wall.

In 1929 the Ministry of Works carried out major strengthening and underpinning work on the tower as well as repointing it using an experimental technique. Again, however, these changes did not fundamentally alter the appearance and the basic character of the church, inside and out, has remained relatively unaltered over the past century.

---

[6] James Gillespie's report 1884 HR59/12/204

An excellent collection of 19th and 20th century photographs has been built up[7]. These have helped with interpretation but have been omitted from this report which focussed upon the medieval building and the period of its destruction.

---

[7] Due mainly to the efforts of Bill Fiet and Dr Mima Magna of the Markinch Heritage Group

Conclusion

The project has achieved it primary aim to chart the development of one of the earliest churches in Scotland for which we have documentary evidence. It has been carried out using a mix of professional and volunteer effort within the framework of a Heritage Lottery funded Landscape Programme and with support from the Strathmartine Trust and Hunter Archaeological and Historical Trust. The direction of future archaeological research has been set out.

As regards the actual building that was gifted around 1050 by the Bishop of St Andrews to the Céli Dé on Loch Leven we have as yet found little trace, but from assembled circumstantial evidence we believe its remains to be underneath the present church at the eastern end. Moreover, it is likely to have been gifted by Scotland's premier Bishop at around the same time as land at Kirkness belonging to Gruoch, MacBeth's wife, was donated to the same religious order. There is an interesting hypothesis that the gift was for

prayers to be said during a visit to Rome by the King and his churchmen[1]. The likelihood that Gruoch was of the MacDuff family[2] and the later links between that family and Markinch (as well as other land gifted at that time) would tend to add some weight to this theory.[3]

The study has, however, focussed upon the gathering of empirical evidence. With respect to the later church that once adjoined the present day tower, a significant amount more is known following the survey of the building. Using the raggle lines on the tower and radar survey under the present day church the survey has succeeded in outlining the three dimensional shape of a nave and chancel that no longer exist in their complete form. The survey has not succeeded in conclusively identifying a particular construction date. This will have to await more sophisticated scientific analysis and a debate between experts in a range of disciplines which we hope this study will bring about. All that can be said at present is that it is most likely to have been built in the first half of the 12th century and may be as early as the first decades of that century in the reigns of Edgar or Alexander I. The reason for the building's existence, however, has been firmly tied in to the MacDuff family and their nearby place of legal assembly.

The project has partially revealed a tower arch that is very simple in style and unstepped both on the side facing into the nave and on the side facing into the tower. The lower stages of the arch facing east, hidden by modern plaster and lathing, have yet to be studied. We now know that the original door to the tower stair was from within the building and that the small elevated northern door was a later insertion. We now have three and possibly four sections of hood moulding from a chancel arch decorated with a saltire design. A double lozenge or diamond string course appears to have stretched around the nave as well as the tower. The picture is incomplete as most of the nave and chancel are now lost but it is difficult to classify the building alongside better preserved later 12th century church buildings such as Dalmeny and Leuchars with their elaborate chevron designs.

Had the building of these churches been contemporaneous with Markinch then, given the high status within Scotland of the MacDuff family, we would

[1] Watson, F. 2010

[2] Woolf, Alex 2007 (p247)

[3] Taylor, S with Márkus, 2012 G. Place Names of Fife, Vol V   p106

have expected much more residual or recycled stone displaying complex design features. Instead we find a simple lozenge design on the tower and nave, four examples of a common chip-cut design from the chancel arch and a tower arch that was apparently unadorned with the exception of a now vanished impost. The external decorated frieze or string course at Markinch is a feature of both Leuchars and Dalmeny but the builder of Markinch, given his status and likely royal connections, is more likely to have imported skills and ideas directly from southern England or even France. This opens up the possibility that Markinch was built early in the 12th century, and the charter evidence, such as it is, also points in this direction.

Although the imposts and dado moulding around the tower arch have been removed, we have found the remains of the hood moulding from another decorated arch of some size. The chip-cut carving matched a series of reused stones on the front of the building. The motif is to be found in Normandy, England and Scotland from the late 11th century until the middle of the 12th century. It appears to have gradually gone out of fashion during the 12th century as chevron work, not so far found at Markinch, increased in popularity.

We have several 12th century towers in Scotland but comparisons sit better with earlier church towers in England, particularly those with simple tower arches. Perhaps at the time Markinch tower was built there were more in Scotland including the now vanished building under Dunfermline Abbey Church. Dunblane in its original state and Muthill may be earlier than Markinch but they appear to have been converted later from secular to ecclesiastical use. The lesser quality of Dunning's stonework need not indicate an earlier construction date than Markinch but simply reflect the availability of a skilled building team or the resources and status of the builder.

Over 800 stonemasons' marks have been recorded and what appears to be the traces of a wheel crane have been measured and logged. The marks give some indication of seasonal activity on the tower and are significantly different from marks surveyed at Leuchars and Dalmeny. These suggest that the overlap of marks between the three buildings was not significant, indicating different teams of masons or a significant time gap between construction, most probably the latter. For the first time it has been possible using style of application as well as form and shape to attribute a single mark to a single individual on different parts of the tower, although this specific mark applied by the individual in question was not found on the other buildings surveyed. One of this mason's stones was also marked with what we interpret as a diagram showing how to lay stones using the half-bonding technique. This emphasises the innovative nature of this form of construction at the time the tower was built.

A parallel survey of overall design features in churches in Eastern Scotland and Northern England found many parallels in terms of decoration and style but no clear pattern of sequential development emerged. A few parallels were found with high status churches in southern England and even Normandy but this served to widen the period within which the building could have been constructed rather than narrowing it.

Features on the tower were identified that to some writers have suggested a mid or even late 12th century construction such as the decorated string course and the treatment of the belfry windows. This study concludes, however, that although it took time for these design features to filter down the social scale into parish churches, examples can be found on high status buildings of the early 12th century. The issue then becomes whether Markinch was an ordinary parish church built in the mid to late 12th century or something out of the ordinary from an earlier part of that century using imported skills. The quality of the build suggests the latter.

A comparison between Markinch and St Rules found significant points of difference in terms of design, construction and function despite their well recognised similarities. This suggests that each should be treated individually in terms of provenance rather than one being seen as a successor to the other. If the building of St Rules is to be ascribed to Bishop Robert then we might consider the possibility that St Rules was built to be grander in all respects to Markinch as would befit a national shrine. This would of course imply that the building at Markinch preceded the supposed shrine at St Andrews. The high quality of the stonework on both buildings need not necessarily imply the same workforce or master mason but might indicate competitive building between two powerful patrons. Much more work is required to compare the two buildings.

The type of lozenge decoration found on Markinch's string courses was found throughout the British Isles but with a concentration in Scotland. However, the poor quality of the preserved lozenge decorated string course at Markinch makes it difficult to compare. Further work is required on the symbolic significance of the lozenge shape, particularly to the early Scottish church.

Difficulty in dating by means of architectural decoration turned our attention towards examining some of the possible builders using charter evidence. The historical analysis suggests that the patron was most likely secular rather than ecclesiastical and points to the MacDuff earls of Fife or clan chiefs styled MacDuff as likely patrons, a family at the apex of the Scottish nobility. Once again, no definitive conclusion could be reached on dating using this historical method but the evidence assembled suggested that the building was likely to have been complete by 1166-67 when it was donated to St Andrews Priory and probably by c1153 when the revenue of its predecessor church was gifted by the Bishop of St Andrews to David I's new priory. This would point towards the three earliest known earls of Fife, Constantine, Gillemichael and Duncan I with Constantine being the most likely candidate if the tower at Markinch preceded that at St Andrews. Both of the recorded secular donors of the 1160s could trace their rights in the building back to Constantine or Gillemichael.

If, as we believe, a member of the MacDuff family built a substantial Anglo-Norman style church in the half century before 1153 then Bishop Robert's gift in that year to the new priory of some cheeses and a pig would represent only that share of the church's overall revenue that he had the right to dispose of. This must have been tied in to the stake he had in the old church gifted by his predecessor a hundred years earlier. We will never know whether Earl Duncan I intended to contribute the church itself and its presumably more substantial lay revenues as he died a year later and the matter was not revived until 1166/67. The picture is complicated by the possibility that the old church was left standing and used as a chancel whilst the new one was being built. By the time the rebuilt church along with its additional supporting revenue was donated, both the bishopric and the earldom had changed hands. The donation, made during the episcopacy of Robert's successor, is recorded separately in the name of three different donors and the claims of each has been assessed in turn.

A possible but unlikely 1160s date for building means that we cannot completely rule out Aedh I as builder. He was probably the MacDuff clan Chief who stood in for Duncan I's son during his minority. Directly descended from Earl Gillemichael but barred from the earldom himself by the newly introduced rules of primogeniture, Aedh could have been motivated by the need to demonstrate his status and lineage to his kinsmen. His role in the building was considered less likely than one of the earls and he would have had little time to complete the project during the minority of Duncan II. It is, however, considered possible that he and his son could have been secular priests of the church ensuring that St Andrews Priory did not get full possession until well into the 13th century.

Looking back to the years before 1153/54 we have to seriously consider Earl Duncan I of Fife as builder, perhaps with the active encouragement and assistance of David I as he attempted to create a model fiefdom in Strathleven for Duncan on the Anglo-Norman model. We know that Duncan was responsible for building at North Berwick and near Earlsferry and he had a relatively long earldom (1133-1154) to accomplish the Markinch project. However, what little we know about Duncan I suggests a Kilconquhar or Rires estate rather than Markinch in the heart of Fife. We found no evidence to connect Duncan I to Markinch although it might be suspected that one or more of his kinsmen held land in the shire of Strathleven around Markinch for either feudal or kinship obligations.

As suggested above, an early date for the church would suggest that it may have been built by either Gillemichael or Constantine the two immediate predecessors of Duncan I. Constantine, was Mormaer from around 1095, Earl, Clan Chief and Senior Scottish law officer. Again, however, evidence is scant, although a senior lawman building a prestigious church close to a traditional legal centre is worth noting. He was a man whose experience and standing in the native aristocracy would have been invaluable to a newly crowned David struggling to secure his kingdom. He is also likely to have been close to David's brothers and predecessors, especially Alexander, king between 1107 and 1124. Records also show that he was personally admired by the monks of Loch Leven as a judge, and other unrecorded secular judgements may have increased his personal wealth.

A parallel may reasonably be drawn between Constantine and Roger of Sarum, Bishop of Salisbury between 1102 and 1139. He was Justiciar of England during the king's absence in France and, through his office, acquired the resources to build many fine castles. The possibility presents itself that Constantine could have begun a prestige project that was completed by his successor, Gillemichael, the grandfather of one of the donors. This could account for the fact that Gillemichael's grandson and Constantine's probable grandson were joint donors in 1166/67 alongside the Bishop of St Andrews.

We do not know how close Constantine was to the royal circle but the privileges bestowed upon his predecessor by Malcolm and Margaret put the MacDuffs upon a pedestal above the rest of the Scottish nobility.[4] Ideas, and even skilled master masons, would have been circulating in the Scottish court well before David I came to the throne. Matilda of Scotland as Queen of England was embarking upon an English church building programme during the reign of her brother King Alexander I (1107-1122). Robert, as Prior of Scone had imported builders around 1115 to construct the now lost priory at Scone. There was probably building work at Selkirk going on around this time. Might the building have emanated from the south of England or even from the heart of Normandy? The Anglo-Norman style in Scotland need not have waited for the arrival of David I or even the completion of Durham Cathedral.

In a cultural sense Fife may have been even closer to the south of England than Yorkshire or Northumberland in the late 11th and early 12th centuries as a result of the connections between the two royal courts and the elites that surrounded them. Additionally, Scotland was spared the devastation suffered by many parts of Northern England as a result of Norman aggression. Building designs, ideas and work teams could arrive relatively quickly in geographically remote areas without a long process of transmission up through the British mainland. Cormac's Chapel in the centre of Ireland, a securely dated building to between 1124 to 1134, shows the level of sophistication that could be achieved by a powerful member of a native aristocracy in a relatively remote corner on the fringes of Europe. By the 1130s there was even a cathedral under construction in far away Orkney, and the building of Trondheim Cathedral was well advanced. Skilled builders and master craftsmen would also have been required for the Anglo-Norman castle building programme during the latter decades of the 11th and the early decades of the 12th centuries.

All this indicates that currently, however much we try to narrow down the dating of the church tower at Markinch, the likely wealth, influence and royal

---

[4] John of Fordun and Andrew of Wynton attest to this from separate sources but no contemporary records remain.

connections of Earl Constantine mean that we cannot eliminate this early part of the 12th century as a strong possibility. This is especially true when we look at the style and quality of building that could be constructed by the elites in Normandy and England in the early 1100s. There is no part of Markinch tower that would have been out of place architecturally in the early decades of the 12th century if we take a European perspective. This includes the decorated string course (a feature even of remote Cashel in the 1120s), the chip-cut carving on the chancel hood-moulding (present on many late 11th century Anglo-Norman churches), the belfry windows reflecting late 11th century Norman stone work and the plain double voussoir tower arch with echoes of Saxo-Norman towers. Unfortunately, as far as dating is concerned, these features are also found later in the century, usually accompanied by innovative design features such as chevron voussoirs. The presence of chevrons at Markinch would have indicated a mid or late 12th century date (as at Dalmeny or Leuchars) but their absence cannot prove an early date. That said, the 19th century antiquarian who set aside the example of the chip-carved section of the old chancel arch when the church was being enlarged would surely have saved distinctive pieces of chevron decoration had they been found at the time. The engaged foliate capital recycled in the 19th century Session House may have been salvaged by the same antiquarian.

We have learned a lot about the building and its possible patrons during the course of the survey but a firm date for its construction will remain illusive in the absence of further survey work. It will require archaeological techniques to test out some of the ideas put forward in the earlier chapters. The carbon dating of samples taken from within the mortar proved unsuccessful on this occasion but experts consulted are convinced that the method will yield indicative results if the correct samples can be obtained. Further archaeological work within the church on the east facing side of the tower as well as under and around the former chancel is also likely to produce significant results. The removal of a sample of plaster from the east side of the tower arch should increase our knowledge about the architectural design features of the building and perhaps even identify traces of original paintwork. There is also the likelihood of significant discoveries being made in the north east corner of the churchyard, a likely dumping ground for building rubble.

With reference to a single building, this 360 degree approach has provided a record for future studies to build upon. There are many other Scottish churches that could be better understood through a multidisciplinary approach combining history, archaeology and art history. It is also hoped also that the attempt to link a specific builder with a particular building has given some insights into how an important section of the Scottish Gaelic elite adopted and adapted Anglo-Norman architectural styles during the dynasty of Malcolm III and Margaret.

The study focussed upon the 12th century but the opportunity was taken to follow through the history of the building's development to later centuries when some now vanished work was undertaken by Prior Hepburn early in the 16th century. Post-Reformation building transformed the church, first by extending the building to the south most probably in the late 17th century and then by extending it to the north in two phases during the 19th century. These extensions were radical but appear to have left relatively intact the east gable of the old chancel and the west gable of the old nave as well as the tower. This is a remarkable degree of survival in a church and tower that may prove to be the oldest building in Scotland still in continuous use.

BIBLIOGRAPHY

Aitcheson, Nick. 2006. Forteviot. *A Pictish and Scottish Royal Centre*. Tempus Publishing Ltd

Alexander, Jennifer S. 2007 *The Introduction and Use of Masons' Marks in Romanesque Buildings* in Medieval Archaeology, 51 2007

Ash, M. , Cunningham, I.C. and Scott W.W. *Syllabus of Scottish Cartularies*, St Andrews in Thomson, T (ed) 1841 BCl.

Bagimond's Roll. ed A.I. Dunlop, SHS Misc 1939

Balgonie Feu Book 1813-1823 University of St Andrews GB 227msDA880.F4B2

Balgonie and Markinch Barony Court Book 1683-1746: Edin. Univ Special
　　　Collections GB/NNAF/C355

Bannerman, John.1993 *MacDuff of Fife* in A. Grant and K. Stringer. Edinburgh University Press

Barclay, Gordon. *Balfarg. The Prehistoric Ceremonial Complex* . Glenrothes Devt. Corp.

Barrow, G.W.S. *The Earls of Fife in the 12th century PSAS* 87

Barrow G.W.S. 1973 *Kingdom of the Scots (pp 237, 238, 271)*. Edinburgh University Press

Barrow G.W.S. 1981 *Kingship and Unity, Scotland 1000-1306*. Edinburgh University Press

Barrow, G.W.S. (ed) *The Acts of William I, 1165-1214*. University Press Edinburgh

Barrow, G. W. S. 1999 The Charters of David I

Bates, D. (ed) *Anglo-Norman Studies XXXV: Proceedings of the Battle Conference 2012 (*esp. article by Alice Taylor on Scottish Law)

Baylé, Maylis, 1979 *La Trinité de Caen*

Beam, A., Bradley, J., Broun, D., Davies, J. R., Hammond, M., Pasin M. (with others), *The People of Medieval Scotland*, 1093 – 1314 (Glasgow and London, 2012),

Bethune of Balfour papers 1511-1900. University of St Andrews, ms 37860

Bennett, G.P. 1988 *Social Conditions Around the Lomonds*, 1775-1875

Bennett, G.P. *The Past at Work around the Lomonds* Markinch Printing Company.

Binding, Günter. 2001 *Medieval Building Techniques.* Tempus Publishing

Blaeu 1654 *Atlas Novus* in the Blaeu Atlas of Scotland, Birlinn/NLS 2006

Blaeu (Gordon), 'Fifae Vicecomitatus, The Sherifdom of Fyfe' James Gordon's map of Fife completed 1645 and published 1654

Blew, William. *"Breviarum Aberdonenses"* 1926

Brooke, C. N. L. 1999 *Churches and Churchmen in Medieval Europe*

Brown, Michael. 2004 *The Wars of Scotland* Edinburgh University Press

Bryden, Rev J.H. 1920 *Memories of Holywood and Markinch*

Cameron, Neil. 1994 *St Rule's Church, St Andrews, and early stone-built Churches in Scotland PSAS 124 (1994)*

Carver, Martin 2008. *Portmahomack Monastery of the Picts.* Edinburgh University Press

Charters of the Hospital of Soltre, of Trinity College Edinburgh BC

Calendar of Entries in the Papal Registers (1.Papal letters and 2. Petitions to the Pope)

Charter of the Burgh of Barony of Markinch 1673. Fife Council

Child, Mark. 2004. *Church Architecture, A Glossary of Terms*

Clarke, David et al. 2012. Early Medieval Scotland. National Museums Scotland

Coldstream, Nicola. *Medieval Craftsmen, Masons and Sculptors*

Conyers L. and Kamp-Whittaker A. 2009 *Results of the Tophane Area GPR Surveys, Bursa, Turkey*

Coppola, G. and Marin, J-Y. *Les Signes Lapidaires sur les Monuments de Caen (XIe - XIIe s) Revue Archeol. Ouest 7 1990 pp 101-109*

Cowan, I. B. & Easson, D. E. *1976 Medieval Religious Houses. Scotland. (Second edn.)*

Crawford, Barbara E. (Ed.) 1988 *St Magnus Cathedral and Orkney's 12th Century Renaissance AUP*

Creighton, O. H. 2002 *Castles and Landscapes* Equinox

Cunningham, A. S. 1907 *Markinch and its Environs*

Cunningham, A. S. 1906 *Kennoway and the Fringes of Markinch*

Curl, James S. 2006 *Oxford Dictionary of Architecture*

Dawson, Jane 2007. *Scotland Re-Formed 1488-1587* Edinburgh University Press

Donaldson, G. 1985 Scottish Church History

Dowden, J. *The Medieval Church in Scotland* (1910)

Du Chesne, André. 1639. *Histoire Généalogique de la maison de Bethune.* Paris

Duncan, A.A.M., *The Foundation of St Andrews Cathedral Priory, 1140,* in The Scottish Historical Review, vol 84, (April, 2005)

Dunlop, Eileen. 2005 *Queen Margaret of Scotland.* NMSE Publishing

Fawcett, Richard. 1997 *Scottish Abbeys and Priories* Historic Scotland

Fawcett, Richard. 1997. *Scottish Cathedrals* Historic Scotland

Fawcett, Richard. 2002 *Scottish Medieval Churches* Tempus

Fawcett, Richard. 2011 *The Architecture of the Scottish Medieval Church.* Yale University Press

Fernie, E.C. 1986 *Early Church Architecture in Scotland,*

Fernie, F. C. 2002. *The Architecture of Norman England*

Fiet, William. 1998 *Old Markinch.*

Fife Court Book, '*The Sheriff Court Book of Fife 1515-22'* Dickinson (ed) 1928 *SHS*

Fife Heritage Series. *Medieval Abbeys and Churches of Fife*

Fraser, James. 1836 plan of Balbirnie and other estates belonging to Lt Gen. Balfour

Fraser, W. (ed) *1890 The Melville Earls of Melville and the Leslies Earls of Leven*

Fraser, W. (ed) 1888 *Memorials of the Family of Wemyss of Wemyss* (3 vols)

Gifford, J. 1988 *The Buildings of Scotland : Fife.* Pevsner Architectural Guides series

Gifford, J. 2007 *The Buildings of Scotland : Perth and Kinross.* Pevsner Architectural Guides series

Gimpel, Jean 1980. *Les Bâtisseurs de Cathédrales*

Gourlay, Ian and Wilkie, Ken. 2001 *The Church in Markinch*

Gourlay, Ian and Wilkie, Ken. 2010 *Markinch, It's Church and Parish*

Green, Lionel. 2013. *Building St Cuthbert's Shrine. Durham Cathedral and the Life of Prior Turgot*

Hannay, R. K. *1913. Rentale Sancti Andree*

Hay, G. 1957. *The Architecture of Scottish Post-Reformation Churches 1560-1843* Oxford

Henderson, Edward, *The History of Lochoreshire*

Henry, Francoise. 1966 L'Art Irlandaise. Zodiaque

Herkless, J. & Hannay R.K. 1913. The Archbishops of St Andrews

Higham, R.& Barker P. 1992 *Timber Castles* Exeter Press

Historic Scotland. *Interim Statements for Cultural Significance for Dunblane, Dunning and Dunfermline..*

Monument Condition Surveys for Dunning, Dunblane and Dunfermline.

Hunter Derek R, 1984 *Markinch Parish Church, 1400 Years of Religious Worship*

Inventory of Writs of the Lands of Balbirnie. Unclassified MSS National Archives

Kerr, Andrew. 1882. *Description of the Ecclesiastical Remains Existing Upon St Serf's Island, Lochleven. PSAS*

Lamont, J. Lamont's Diary *The Diary of Mr John Lamont of Newton 1649-71*

Lamont-Brown, R. 1988 *Discovering Fife*

Lawrie, Archibald (ed). 1905 *Early Scottish Charters,*

Leighton, John. 1840 *History of the County of Fife*

Leslie-Melville Muniments. National Archives for Scotland. (heritors' minutes HR59)

Leslie-Melville Archives , Univ. of St Andrews GB 0227 msDA880.F4B21

Liddiard, R. 2003 Anglo-Norman Castles

McAleer, J. P. *The West Front of Durham Cathedral.* in Rollason, D. et al. 1998

Macfarlane, W. 1900 *Genealogical Collections concerning Families in Scotland* SHS

MacFarlane, W. 'Geographical Collections relating to Scotland' in A. Mitchell, A.& Toshach, J. (eds) SHS 1908

MacGibbon, David and Ross, Thomas, 1896-7. *The ecclesiastical architecture of Scotland from the earliest Christian times to the seventeenth century, 3 vols.*

MacGregor, A. R. 1996 *Fife and Angus Geology.* Pentland Press

MacQuarrie, Alan. 2004. *Medieval Scotland* Sutton

MacQuarrie Alan. 1985. *Scotland and the Crusades.* Edinburgh John Donald

McCallum, John. *The Reformation in Fife, 1560-1640.* PhD Thesis

McDonald, Andrew. 2003. *Outlaws of Medieval Scotland.* Tuckwell Press

MacKay, Æ. J. G. (1896) T*he History of Fife and Kinross*

Manson, Bruce. 2010 *Fife, Why a Kingdom? The Historical Roots of Regional Identity* FC

Manson, Bruce 2010 *Markinch, A Historic Tour of the Town and its Buildings. MHG*

Marquis de Ruvigny and Raineval, 1902 *Moutrie of Seafield and Roscobie,*

Marsden, John 2010. *Kings, Mormaers, Rebels. Early Scotland's Other Royal Family* Birlinn

Martin, M. (updated 2016) The Fife Pits and Memorial Book (online) www.fifepits.co.uk

Mercer, R.J. et al. '*The Neolithic Henge-Type Enclosure at Balfarg*'. Proc Soc Antiq 1988

Millar, A.H. 1895 *Fife, Pictorial and Historical* (2 vols)

Millar, Lieut. Col. 'An Enquiry concerning the site of the Battle of Mons Graupius', Archaeologica Scotica 4.

Munro, David. 1994 *Loch Leven and the River Leven, A Landscape Transformed*

Musset, Lucien. 1975. *Normandie Romane.* Zodiaque

News from the Past, Markinch Heritage Group Newsletter. (various articles on the church's history) National Library of Scotland

Nimmo, Bill. 2012. A Guide to Old St Andrews Kirk, Gullane

North Berwick Cartulary. *Bannatyne Club* 1847

O'Grady, Dr Oliver J. T. 2013. *Markinch Parish Church, Report on Geophysical Survey*

O'Keeffe, T. (2003) *Romanesque Ireland: architecture and ideology in the twelfth century,* Academia

O'Keefe, T. *Lismore and Cashel: Reflections on the Beginnings of Romanesque Architecture in Munster.* The Journal of the Royal Society of Antiquaries of Ireland Vol. 124 (1994), pp. 118-152

Ordnance Survey Name Books for Fife and Kinross-shire

Oram, Richard. 2002. *The Canmores* Tempus

Oram, Richard. 2004. *David I, the King who made Scotland* Tempus

Oram, Richard. 2005. *Lordship and Architecture in Medieval and Renaissance Scotland.* Birlinn

Oram, Richard. 2011. *Domination and Lordship, Scotland 1070-1230* Edinburgh University Press

Ousel, Raymond. 1968. *Bourgogne Romane.* Zodiaque

Parochial Directory for Markinch 1861

Parsons, David All Saints Church Brixworth, Northamptonshire: The Development of the Fabric *c.* 1100 to 1865

Pearson T. and Ainsworth S. Norham Castle. English Heritage Survey Report 2002

Pitcairn, Constance. 1905 *The History of the Fife Pitcairns*

Places of Worship in Scotland
SCHR *http://www.scottishchurches.org.uk*

Potter, John F. 2009. *Patterns of Stonework: The Early Church in Britain and Ireland.* BAR 496

Pride, G.L. 1990 *The Kingdom of Fife, An Illustrated Architectural Guide.* Rutland Press

Proudfoot, Edwina. Scottish Church Heritage Research Newsletter

Regiam Majestatem. in *Stair Society* 1947

Register of the Great Seal. Thomson J.M. et al, 1882-1914

Rodwell, Warwick. 2012 *The Archaeology of Churches.* Amberley

Rollason, D., Harvey, M., & Prestwich M. 1994. *Anglo-Norman Durham 1093-1193.* Boydell Press

Rollason, D., Piper, A. J., Harvey, M. Rollason L. 2004. *The Durham Liber Vitae and its Context*

Ross, Alisdair 2011 *The Kings of Alba* Birlinn

Rowntree Bodie, W.G. 1968 *Some Light on the Past Around Glenrothes*

Rowntree Bodie W. G. *Glenrothes and its Environs in Days Gone By*

Roy, Wm. The Military Survey of Scotland, 1747-55. NLS online service

Russell, John R. 1882 The Kingdom - A Descriptive and Historical Handbook to Fife.

Russell-White, C.J. 'Medieval Features and Finds from Balfarg/Balbirnie, Fife'. *Proc Soc Antiq Scot*

Sanderson, Margaret 2001. *Cardinal of Scotland, David Beaton* John Donald Publishers

Scotichronicon by Walter Bower (9 vols) Watt, D.E.R. (ed)

Schofield, J. and Lea, R. 2005. *Holy Trinity Priory, Aldgate, City of London.* Molas monograph 24. Museum of London

Seivewright, Rev J. Second Statistical Account for Markinch parish (1834-45)

Sharratt, France and Peter. 1985. *Écosse Romane.* Photographies inédites de Zodiaque.

Sheriff Court of Fife Deeds 1715-1809

Sibbald, Robert. *The History Ancient and Modern of the Sheriffdoms of Fife and Kinross* 1710. (Cupar edition 1803)

Smith, R.A.L. 2005 *History of the Clan Lundy. Lundie, Lundin*

Smyth, Alfred P. *Warlords and Holy Men.* Edward Arnold

State of Title Deeds of the various properties now belonging to John Balfour Esq. of Balbirnie. Manuscript Folio with Jean Balfour, Kirkforthar.

Stevenson, W. *The Presbytrie Booke of Kirkcaldie 1630 - 1653*

Stevenson Rev. W. 1882 *A Historical Account of the Kirk and Kirk Session of Markinch*

Stringer, K. J. 1985. *Earl David of Huntingdon - A Study in Anglo-Scottish History* Edinburgh University Press

Taylor, A. 2016. *The Shape of the State in Medieval Scotland 1124 - 1290*

Taylor H. M. & Taylor J. (3 vols 1965, 1978) *Anglo Saxon Architecture*

Taylor, J.W. *Historical Antiquities of Fife, Chiefly Ecclesiastical*

Taylor, Robert. 1811. *The Markinch Minstrelsy*

Taylor, Simon (ed) 2000. *Kings, Clerics and Chronicles in Scotland, 500-1297* Four Courts Press

Taylor, Dr. Simon. 2009 Knowing your Place. A Place-Name Walk in Fife

Taylor, Dr. Simon with Gilbert, Márkus. *The Place-Names of Fife.* Vol II 2010. **This is the major source of local bibliographic material and cross references to local historical material**

Taylor, Dr. Simon with Gilbert, Márkus. *The Place-Names of Fife.* Vol V

Thomson, David. *Plan of Markinch 1765.* Redrawn with additions 1854, FCA, Tullis Russell Archives

Thomson, J. 1791 *Statistical Account of the Parish of Markinch (OSA)*

Torrie, Rev. A.R.R. 1958 *In the Steps of St Brendan* Northern Scot

Turner, S, Semple S. & Turner A. 2013 *Wearmouth and Jarrow. Northumbrian Monasteries in a Historic Landscape*

Veitch, Kenneth *Replanting Paradise : Alexander I and the Reform of Religious Life in Scotland* Innes Review Vol 52 No 2 2001

Walker, Ian. 2006. *Lords of Alba* Sutton Publishing

Walker, J. Russell. 1895. *Pre-Reformation Church Architecture in Fifeshire*

Watson, Fiona. 2010 *MacBeth, A True Story*

Webb, Simon. 2010 *In Search of Bede*

Webster, Rev. J. M. 1948 *Dunfermline Abbey.* Carnegie Dunfermline Trust.

Wilkie, James 1931 *Bygone Fife*

Wood, A.J.D. 1988 *40 Years New, Glenrothes 1948-1988*

Wyntoun, Andrew of, *The Original Chronicle (from Cottonian and Wemyss mss http://digital.nls.uk/106458535*

Woolf, Alex. 2007. *From Pictland to Alba 789-1070* Edinburgh University Press

Yeoman, Peter. 1999. *Pilgrimage in Medieval Scotland. Historic Scotland*

Young, Alan. 1997. *The Comyns, 1212-1324* Tuckwell Press

Zupko, R. E. 1977. British Weights & Measures: A History From Antiquity to the Seventeenth Century.

Websites

A number of websites have been consulted including :-

arts.st-andrews.ac.uk/corpusofscottishchurches/ A Corpus of Scottish Medieval Parish Churches [accessed 2015 - 2016]

www.scottishchurches.org.uk Places of Worship in Scotland [accessed 2015] www.crsbi.ac.uk Corpus of Romanesque Sculpture for Britain and Ireland [accessed 2015 - 2016]

POMS - Amanda Beam, John Bradley, Dauvit Broun, John Reuben Davies, Matthew Hammond, Michele Pasin (with others), The People of Medieval Scotland, 1093 – 1314 (Glasgow and London, 2012), www.poms.ac.uk. [accessed 2016]

Models of Authority ; Scottish Charters and the Emergence of Government 1100-1250 modelsofauthority.ac.uk

Unpublished Theses and Reports

Hammond, M. H. *A Prosopographical Analysis of Society in East Central Scotland* PhD Univ. of Glasgow 2005

Markinch Burials 1799 to 1854 (online)

Maidment Templaria 1829 from a collection held by Ferguson, Andrew, Unpublished draft

 Manson, B. 2015. *Stonemasons' Working Practices A Comparison of 12th Century Churches in the East of Scotland (unpub)*

Manson, Bruce. 2008 *The Landholdings of Markinch*

Manson, Bruce. 2008 *Medieval Markinch and Dalginch. Historical and Landscape Background to 2008 Excavation.* (unpub.)

Manson, Bruce 2008 *The Terraces of Markinch Hill.* (unpub.)

Manson, Bruce. 2009 *Markinch Church. The Building and its Historical Development* (unpub.)

Manson, Bruce. 2008 *The Moutries, Lords of Markinch and Neighbours from Hell*

O'Grady, Oliver J.T. (2008) *The setting and practice of open-air judicial assemblies in medieval Scotland: a multidisciplinary study.* PhD thesis. Univ. of Glasgow

Semple, Dr M-C. 2009 A*n Archaeology of Scotland's Early Romanesque Churches : The Towers of Alba.* Phd thesis for Glasgow University.

Plans and Drawings

RHP35973/6 Elevation of Markinch Church 1805

RHP35971/1 Plan of Markinch Church 1805

RHP7122 Pictorial sketch of new session house and church tower at Markinch, Fife. 1888

RHP123 Architectural drawings of Markinch parish church, Fife. 1884

RHP123/1 Markinch parish church, Fife: ground plan. 1884

RHP123/2 Markinch parish church, Fife: gallery plan. 1884

RHP123/3 Markinch parish church, Fife: north elevation. 1884

RHP7123/3 Markinch parish church, Fife: east elevation and section. 1884

RHP124 Plan of Markinch glebe, Fife 1886

RHP7125 Plan of proposed excambion at Markinch manse and glebe, Fife. c1901

RHP7126 Architectural drawing of Markinch manse garden, Fife. 1903

RHP7126/1 Markinch manse, Fife: cover of plan. 1903

RHP7126/2 Markinch manse, Fife: block plan. 1903

RHP7127 Architectural drawing of Markinch parish Church, Fife. 19th c.

RHP7127 Architectural drawing of Markinch parish church, Fife. 19th c.

RHP7129 Architectural drawing of
Markinch parish church, Fife. 19th c.
RHP7130 Architectural drawing of
Markinch parish church, Fife. 19th c.
RHP7131 Architectural drawing of
Markinch parish church, Fife. 19th c.
RHP 7132 Architectural drawing of
Markinch parish church, Fife. 19th c.
RHP7133 Architectural drawing of
Markinch parish church, Fife. 19th c.
RHP7134 Architectural drawing of
Markinch parish church, Fife. 19th c.
Drawings and plans of Markinch Church
from the Special Collections Department of
St Andrews University - ms37778b/
335/1-13

Glossary of abbreviations

BCl Bannatyne Club
FC Fife Council
FCA Fife Council Archives
MHG Markinch Heritage group
PSAS proceedings of the Society of
Antiquaries of Scotland
SHS Scottish History Society
YAS Yorkshire Archaeological Society
RRS The Register of the Privy Seal of
Scotland
St A Lib The Book of Charters of the Priory
of St Andrews

Index of Key Names and Places